# Mental Models for Kids

*The Illustrated Guide to Thinking Smarter, Learning Faster, and Outsmarting Any Challenge!*

# Table of Contents

# Introduction: The Superpower You Didn't Know You Had!

*Hey there, future genius!*

Have you ever wanted to **think faster, solve tricky problems, and always know the smartest choice to make?** Guess what? You already have a **superpower** — your brain! But here's the secret: **most people don't know how to use their brains in the best way.**

That's where **Mental Models** come in.

## What's a Mental Model?

A mental model is like a **thinking tool** that helps you figure things out. Imagine your brain is a giant **toolbox**. You wouldn't try to build a treehouse with just a spoon, right? You'd want a **hammer, saw, and screwdriver** to help you do the job.

Mental models are like **those tools, but for your brain —** they help you make better choices, learn faster, and solve problems like a detective.

## Why Do You Need Mental Models?

Life is full of challenges, big and small. Here are some examples:

- **You have a HUGE school project**—where do you even start?!
- **You want to save up for something awesome** — but should you spend or wait?

- **You have an argument with a friend** — who's really right?
- **You keep making the same mistake** — how do you fix it?

Mental models help you **outsmart** these challenges. **They are used by scientists, leaders, and even superheroes (yep, Batman uses them too!).**

## What You'll Learn in This Book

In this book, you'll discover **50 powerful thinking tools** that will help you:

- **Solve problems faster** (like a detective!)
- **Make smarter choices** (and avoid silly mistakes)
- **Learn anything faster** (like a supercomputer!)
- **Outsmart tricky situations** (even with grown-ups!)

Each chapter will have **fun stories, cool examples, and simple tricks** that you can use **right away** in school, at home, and in everyday life.

By the end, **you'll be thinking like a genius!**

**Are You Ready to Unlock Your Super Brain?**

Let's get started! Turn the page, and **let's outsmart the world!**

# Part 1: Smart Thinking Basics

Did you know your brain is like a **supercomputer**? But just like a computer needs the right apps to work best, your brain needs the **right thinking tools** to solve problems, make good choices, and understand the world. In this part, you'll learn **six powerful ways to think smarter** — like breaking big problems into tiny pieces, spotting the simplest answer, and even **thinking backward** to solve tricky puzzles. Ready to level up your brain? Let's go!

# Chapter 1: First Principles Thinking

Imagine you want to build the **best** paper airplane in the world. You could copy someone else's design, but what if you want to make it fly even farther? Instead of just guessing, you break the problem down to understand **what really makes a plane fly.**

This way of thinking is called **First Principles Thinking**. It means looking at a problem like a scientist — breaking it down to its simplest parts and figuring things out from the ground up, rather than just doing what others have always done.

## How It Works

Instead of assuming something is just the way it is, ask:

- **What are the basic pieces of this problem?**
- **Why does this work the way it does?**
- **How can I make it better?**

This kind of thinking is what inventors and problem-solvers use when they want to create something **new and better** instead of just copying what already exists.

## Example: Building a Treehouse

Emma wants to build a treehouse, but she has never built one before. If she just looks at other treehouses, she might feel stuck because she doesn't know how to make hers strong.

Instead of giving up, she **breaks the problem into simple parts**:

- **What does a treehouse need?** A base, walls, and a roof.
- **What will hold it up?** A strong tree and secure beams.
- **What materials can I use?** Wood, nails, and a hammer.
- **Who can help me?** Maybe a parent, a builder, or a book about construction.

By thinking step by step, Emma **solves the problem instead of getting overwhelmed.**

## How You Can Use First Principles Thinking

This works in **everyday life**, too. Let's say you're struggling with a tough math problem. Instead of saying, "I just don't get it," you break it down:

- **What do I already know?**
- **Which parts are confusing?**
- **Can I try a different way to solve it?**

Or maybe you want to improve at a sport. Instead of copying how everyone else plays, ask:

- **What makes someone really good at this?**
- **What are the key skills I need?**
- **How can I practice smarter?**
- **Why This Matters**

Most people **don't** think like this. They assume things work a certain way just because that's how they've always been. But the smartest people — scientists, inventors, and leaders — use First Principles Thinking to **ask better questions, find better** answers, and create new ideas.

So, next time you're stuck on a problem, **don't just accept the usual way of doing things.** Break it down, understand the basic pieces, and **build your own best solution.**

# Chapter 2: Second-Order Thinking

Imagine you throw a rock into a pond. At first, you see the splash. But if you watch closely, you'll notice ripples spreading out across the water, touching everything around them.

That's exactly how **Second-Order Thinking** works—it's about looking beyond the first result and thinking about what happens *next*.

Most people stop at **first-order thinking**, which is only looking at the immediate effect of a decision. But **smart thinkers** ask:

- **What happens after this?**
- **Will this cause new problems or opportunities?**
- **If I do this now, what will things look like later?**

By thinking a few steps ahead, you can avoid mistakes, make better choices, and even **outsmart problems before they happen.**

## Example: The Homework Trap

Liam has a choice: he can do his homework now or watch his favorite show. He chooses the show, thinking, "It's just one assignment, and I'll do it later." That's first-order thinking — only looking at what happens *right now.*

But what happens next?

- He forgets about the homework.
- The next morning, he's stressed and scrambling to finish it.
- He rushes, makes mistakes, and gets a bad grade.

Now, let's say Liam uses **Second-Order Thinking**. He stops and asks himself, "If I skip my homework now, what will happen later?" He realizes he might get in trouble or feel stressed the next day. So, he decides to finish his work first, then enjoy his show without worry.

## Another Example: The Candy Dilemma

Emma has saved her allowance for weeks. She has enough money to buy a huge bag of candy. Her first thought is, "This will be awesome!" But if she thinks deeper:

- **What happens after I eat all that candy?** She might feel sick.
- **Will I still have money left?** No, she'll have to start saving all over again.
- **What's a smarter choice?** Maybe buying a small treat and saving the rest for something bigger later.

By thinking beyond the *first* outcome, Emma avoids regret and makes a better choice.

## How to Use Second-Order Thinking

Before making a decision, stop and ask:

1. **What happens next?**
2. **Then what?**
3. **And then what?**

This is how **chess players, business leaders, and scientists** make smart moves — they don't just think about now, they think about **five steps ahead.**

## Why This Matters

Many mistakes happen because people **only think about the short term.** But if you start thinking about the **next steps**, you can:

- Avoid bad choices before they happen.
- Make decisions that help you in the long run.
- Stay ahead of problems instead of fixing them later.

So, next time you have a choice to make, **don't just think about today.** Think about **tomorrow, next week, and beyond**!

# Chapter 3: Occam's Razor

Have you ever heard a really complicated explanation for something simple? Maybe your little brother thought aliens stole his missing toy, when really, he just left it under the couch. That's where **Occam's Razor** comes in — it's a thinking tool that helps you find the simplest, most likely answer instead of overcomplicating things.

Occam's Razor says: **"The simplest explanation is usually the right one."** It doesn't mean the simplest answer is *always* correct, but most of the time, it's the best place to start. Instead of adding unnecessary ideas, it helps you focus on what makes the most sense.

### Example: The Case of the Missing Sock

James is getting dressed when he realizes one of his socks is missing. His first thought is, "Maybe my dog stole it and buried it in the backyard, or maybe my little sister took it for a secret project." But before he starts digging up the yard, he stops and asks, **"What's the simplest explanation?"**

- Did he check the laundry basket?
- Could it still be in the dryer?
- Maybe it's just stuck inside another piece of clothing?

After looking in the dryer, James finds the sock stuck to a sweatshirt. The mystery is solved — not by wild guesses, but by checking the most **likely** answer first.

## Another Example: The Late Bus Mystery

Mia's school bus is late. Some of her friends start making wild guesses:

- "Maybe the driver quit and left the bus on the side of the road."
- "What if a famous celebrity needed a ride and took our bus instead?"

Instead of jumping to extreme ideas, Mia thinks, **"What's the simplest reason?"** She realizes the bus is probably stuck in traffic or had to stop for a long red light. A few minutes later, the bus arrives — just like she expected.

## How to Use Occam's Razor

Next time something seems confusing, ask yourself:

1. **What's the simplest explanation?**
2. **Does this make sense based on what I know?**
3. **Am I adding extra details that aren't necessary?**

This helps you avoid **wasting time on complicated guesses** and lets you **focus on the most likely truth.**

## Why This Matters

Occam's Razor helps people **avoid overthinking and making things harder than they need to be.** Scientists use it when solving mysteries about nature, detectives use it when investigating crimes, and you can use it to **think clearly and solve everyday problems faster.**

Remember, before you assume something crazy, **start with the simplest explanation.** It might save you a lot of time and confusion!

# Chapter 4: Hanlon's Razor

Have you ever waved at a friend, but they didn't wave back? Or maybe you raised your hand in class, but the teacher didn't call on you? It's easy to think, **"They're mad at me"** or **"They don't like me."** But what if there was a simpler reason? What if your friend just didn't see you? What if your teacher was busy thinking about the lesson?

That's what **Hanlon's Razor** teaches us. It says: **"Never assume people are trying to hurt you when a mistake or misunderstanding is a more likely reason."**

People aren't perfect. They forget things, they get busy, and sometimes, they just don't realize how their actions affect others. Instead of assuming someone is being mean on purpose, Hanlon's Razor helps you stop, think, and **give people the benefit of the doubt.**

### Example: The Forgotten Birthday

Noah's best friend, Jake, always remembers his birthday. But this year, Jake didn't say anything. Noah feels hurt. **"Did he stop caring about me?"** he wonders.

Before jumping to conclusions, Noah decides to think through it.

- Did Jake seem upset with him lately? No.
- Is it possible Jake just forgot because he's busy? Maybe.
- Could there be another reason? Yes — maybe something is happening in Jake's life that Noah doesn't know about.

Later, Jake texts Noah, **"I feel awful! My grandma was in the hospital, and I completely forgot your birthday. I'm so sorry!"** Noah realizes that Jake wasn't ignoring him on purpose — he just had a lot on his mind.

## Another Example: The Teacher's Mistake

Emma raises her hand in class, but the teacher never calls on her. She feels frustrated. **"Maybe my teacher just doesn't like me!"**

But if Emma uses Hanlon's Razor, she can think of other explanations:

- Maybe the teacher didn't see her hand.
- Maybe there were too many students to call on everyone.
- Maybe the teacher was focused on another part of the lesson.

Instead of assuming the worst, Emma asks her teacher after class. The teacher smiles and says, **"I'm so sorry! I was looking at the other side of the room. I'll make sure to call on you next time."**

## How to Use Hanlon's Razor

Whenever someone upsets you, ask yourself:

1. **Is it possible this was just a mistake?**
2. **Could they be distracted, busy, or not realize what they did?**
3. **What's a more likely explanation than them doing this on purpose?**

Most of the time, people don't mean to hurt us. They're just dealing with their own thoughts, problems, or distractions.

## Why This Matters

Jumping to conclusions can **hurt friendships, create unnecessary arguments, and make us feel bad for no reason.** Hanlon's Razor helps us stay calm, be understanding, and **avoid drama that isn't even real.**

Next time you feel like someone is being unfair or unkind, **pause and think: Could this just be a simple mistake?** It might change the way you see the situation — and make life a lot easier.

# Chapter 5: Inversion

"SOMETIMES FLIPPING THE PROBLEM REVEALS THE SOLUTION."

PROBLEM

OPPOSITE OUTCOME

Imagine you are in a giant maze, trying to find your way out. You could walk forward and hope you don't hit a dead end, but what if you tried something different? What if you imagined **starting from the end** and working backward? That's what **Inversion** is all about — it helps you solve problems by thinking in reverse.

Most people try to figure things out by asking, **"How do I succeed?"** But sometimes, a better question is, **"How do I avoid failure?"** By flipping the problem around, you can find answers you might not have thought of before.

## Example: Becoming a Great Soccer Player

Daniel wants to be the best player on his soccer team. He could focus only on what to do — practicing drills, running faster, and watching professional players. But if he uses Inversion, he asks, **"What would make me a terrible player?"**

He realizes that bad players:

- Skip practice
- Don't listen to their coach
- Get frustrated and give up easily

Now, by avoiding those mistakes, Daniel knows exactly what *not* to do. That makes his path to success much clearer.

## Another Example: Getting a Good Grade on a Test

Sarah has an important test coming up. Instead of just asking, **"How do I get an A?"** she flips the question and asks, **"What would make me fail?"**

She realizes she would fail if she:

- Waited until the last minute to study
- Didn't get enough sleep before the test
- Rushed through the questions without checking her answers

By avoiding these mistakes, Sarah automatically improves her chances of doing well.

## How to Use Inversion

Next time you face a problem, try these steps:

1. Think about the result you want.
2. Flip the problem around and ask, **"What would cause the opposite of what I want?"**
3. Make a list of things to avoid.
4. Use that list to make better decisions.

## Why This Matters

Many people only think about what they *should* do, but they forget to consider what they *shouldn't* do. Inversion helps you avoid common mistakes, plan smarter, and see problems from a new perspective.

Whether you want to do well in school, improve at a sport, or solve a tricky problem, try thinking backward. Sometimes, the best way forward is to start at the end.

# Chapter 6: The Circle of Competence

Nobody knows everything—but everyone is good at *something*. The **Circle of Competence** is about understanding what you *do* know, what you *don't* know, and what you *can* learn. Smart thinkers **focus on their strengths while being honest about their weaknesses.**

Your **Circle of Competence** is like a map of your knowledge. The things inside your circle are what you understand well. The things outside are areas where you might need help or more learning. **The key to smart thinking is knowing the difference.**

### Example: Asking for Help in Math

Sofia is great at writing but struggles with math. She could pretend she understands, but that wouldn't help her. Instead, she thinks:

- **Inside my circle:** I'm good at essays, storytelling, and grammar.
- **Outside my circle:** I need help with fractions and percentages.

Because she knows where she needs improvement, she asks a classmate for help — and soon, her math skills grow!

## Another Example: Fixing a Broken Bike

Noah's bike chain falls off. He wants to fix it himself, but he's never done it before. Instead of guessing, he uses the Circle of Competence:

- **Inside my circle:** I know how to ride and take care of my bike.
- **Outside my circle:** I don't know how to fix the chain *yet.*

So, he watches a tutorial and asks his dad for guidance. **Now, his circle grows—he's learned something new!**

## How to Use the Circle of Competence

1. **Know what you're good at—use it to your advantage.**
2. **Be honest about what you don't know—ask for help when needed.**
3. **Expand your circle by learning new things over time.**

## Why This Matters

The smartest people **aren't the ones who pretend to know everything—they're the ones who know what they *don't* know.** By recognizing your strengths and weaknesses, you can keep growing, keep learning, and **keep getting better every day!**

# Part 2: Learning Superpowers

Have you ever wished learning new things could be easier? Some people seem to pick up skills quickly, while others struggle. But here's the secret: **learning isn't about being "naturally smart." It's about using the right strategies.** In this part, you'll discover thinking tools that help you learn faster, remember more, and improve at anything. Whether it's school, sports, or hobbies, these superpowers will make learning feel less like a chore and more like a game.

# Chapter 7: The Learning Curve

Think about the first time you rode a bike. At first, it felt impossible. You wobbled, lost balance, and maybe even fell. But after practicing for a few days, it got easier. After a few weeks, you barely had to think about it. That's because of something called **The Learning Curve**—a pattern that shows how people improve over time.

At the beginning of learning something new, progress feels **slow and frustrating.** But the more you practice, the **faster and easier** it gets. Understanding this can help you push through the tough part instead of giving up.

### Example: Learning to Play an Instrument

Ethan decides he wants to learn the guitar. He picks it up, strums the strings, and it sounds terrible. His fingers hurt, and the chords are confusing. He starts thinking, **"Maybe I'm just not good at this."**

But if Ethan understands The Learning Curve, he knows that this **slow, difficult phase is completely normal.** The more he practices, the faster his brain and fingers adjust. After a few weeks, playing becomes easier. A few months later, he's playing full songs.

## Another Example: Getting Better at Math

Sofia struggles with long division. The steps feel confusing, and she keeps making mistakes. At first, she thinks, **"I'll never get this."** But instead of giving up, she remembers The Learning Curve.

She realizes:

- **The first part of learning is always the hardest.**
- **Every time she practices, it gets a little easier.**
- **One day, the thing that feels impossible will feel automatic.**

After practicing for a few weeks, long division stops feeling scary. It's not because she suddenly got "smarter" — it's because she gave her brain time to adjust.

## How to Use The Learning Curve

When something feels hard to learn, remind yourself:

1. **Everyone struggles at first.**
2. **The more you practice, the easier it gets.**
3. **If you keep going, what feels impossible today will feel simple later.**

## Why This Matters

Most people quit when something feels too difficult. But The Learning Curve shows that **struggle is just the first step to success.** If you know that learning starts off slow but speeds up over time, you'll have the patience to stick with it — and that's how real learning happens.

# Chapter 8: Feedback Loops

Have you ever played a video game where you keep losing at the same level? At first, it's frustrating, but after a few tries, you start noticing patterns. You figure out where you went wrong, adjust your strategy, and before you know it—you beat the level. That's because of something called a **Feedback Loop** — a powerful tool for getting better at anything.

A **Feedback Loop** happens when you do something, see the results, and use that information to improve. Instead of making the same mistakes over and over, you learn from them and get better each time. The faster you use feedback, the faster you improve.

### Example: Shooting a Basketball

David wants to get better at shooting basketballs into the hoop. At first, he misses most of his shots. If he just keeps throwing the ball without thinking, he won't improve much. But if he **pays attention to what went wrong**, he can adjust:

- If the ball goes too far, he knows to use less force.
- If it's too short, he knows to push a little harder.
- If it's off to the side, he knows to fix his aim.

By making small adjustments each time, David **improves quickly** instead of repeating the same mistakes.

## Another Example: Writing a Story

Emma loves writing, but when she turns in her short story for school, her teacher marks several mistakes. At first, she feels discouraged. But instead of giving up, she **uses the feedback** to improve:

- She fixes the grammar mistakes.
- She adds more details where her teacher said it was confusing.
- She practices writing clearer sentences.

The next time she writes a story, she avoids those same mistakes—and gets a much better grade.

## How to Use Feedback Loops

To improve at anything, follow these steps:

1. **Try something.** Take a shot, write a paragraph, solve a math problem—whatever it is.
2. **See what happens.** Did it work, or did something go wrong?
3. **Adjust and improve.** Change what didn't work, and try again.
4. **Repeat the loop.** The more times you go through the loop, the better you get.

## Why This Matters

Many people fail because they **ignore feedback** or get frustrated by mistakes. But the fastest way to get better at anything is to **pay attention to what works, fix what doesn't, and keep going.** If you use Feedback Loops in learning, sports, and even everyday life, you'll improve **faster than ever.**

# Chapter 9: Meta-Learning

Have you ever watched someone learn something new really fast? Maybe your friend picked up a new video game in minutes or became great at skateboarding in just a few weeks. It might seem like they have some special talent, but in reality, they probably just know how to **learn better.** That's what **Meta-Learning** is—learning how to learn.

Most people focus on what they're learning, but few stop to ask, **"What's the best way to learn this?"** Meta-Learning helps you figure that out so you can learn anything faster and more easily.

## Example: Learning a New Language

Lucas wants to learn Spanish. He could just memorize a long list of words and hope for the best, but that would take forever. Instead, he asks himself, **"What's the best way to learn a language?"**

- He notices that listening to native speakers helps him remember words faster.

- He realizes that practicing speaking every day makes the words stick.
- He finds out that using flashcards helps him learn new words more easily.

Instead of just studying harder, Lucas studies **smarter.** By using the best methods, he improves much faster than someone just trying random approaches.

## Another Example: Preparing for a Test

Sophia needs to study for a big history test. At first, she just reads the textbook over and over, but she isn't remembering much. Instead of getting frustrated, she stops and thinks, **"What's the best way for me to learn this?"**

She tries different methods:

- Writing down key points helps her understand better.
- Teaching the information to her little brother makes her remember it more clearly.
- Taking practice quizzes shows her what she still needs to work on.

Now, instead of just spending more time studying, she's studying the right way — and her grades improve.

## How to Use Meta-Learning

Before you start learning something, ask yourself:

1. **What's the best way to learn this?**
2. **Who has already learned this, and how did they do it?**
3. **Which methods help me learn the fastest?**

## Why This Matters

Most people waste time using slow, ineffective ways of learning. But when you understand how to **learn better**, you can improve at anything — school subjects, sports, hobbies, or even life skills. Instead of just working harder, **work smarter** by finding the best way to learn.

# Chapter 10: Incremental Growth

Have you ever seen a tree grow? If you watch it for just a day, it looks like nothing is happening. But over weeks, months, and years, that tiny tree turns into something tall and strong. Learning and improving work the same way. **Small efforts add up over time, even if you don't see results right away.** This is called **Incremental Growth** — getting better little by little until big changes happen.

Many people give up on learning because they don't see quick progress. But the truth is, **every small improvement adds up, even if it feels slow at first.**

### Example: Running Faster

Ben wants to get better at running. On his first try, he runs for five minutes and feels exhausted. He could think, **"I'll never be good at this,"** but instead, he decides to improve just a little each day.

- The next day, he runs for six minutes.
- A week later, he reaches ten minutes.
- A month later, he can run for twenty minutes without stopping.

He didn't become a great runner overnight. **By improving just a little each time, he slowly built up his skill.**

## Another Example: Becoming a Better Reader

Mia struggles with reading. The long words and big paragraphs make her feel frustrated. Instead of quitting, she decides to practice just a little bit each day.

- She starts by reading one short page every night.
- A few weeks later, she moves to two pages.
- After a couple of months, she can read full chapters without struggling.

At first, she didn't notice much progress, but over time, those small efforts **turned her into a confident reader.**

## How to Use Incremental Growth

When trying to get better at something, remember:

1. **You don't need to improve all at once — just a little bit at a time.**
2. **Even small efforts add up if you keep going.**
3. **What feels hard today will feel easy in the future if you stay consistent.**

## Why This Matters

Most people give up because they don't see instant results. But **big success comes from small improvements over time.** Whether you're learning a skill, getting stronger, or improving at school, **focus on getting just a little better each day — and one day, you'll be amazed at how far you've come.**

# Chapter 11: Shoshin (Beginner's Mind)

Little kids ask a lot of questions. They're always curious, wondering how things work and why things happen. That's because they have something called **Shoshin, or Beginner's Mind** — a way of thinking that helps people stay open to learning, no matter how much they already know.

Many people, as they get older, stop being curious. They think they already understand everything, so they stop asking questions and trying new ideas. But the smartest people in the world **keep a Beginner's Mind their whole lives.** They never assume they know everything, and because of that, they keep learning and discovering new things.

### Example: The Chess Player Who Stopped Improving

Lucas is great at chess. He wins most of his games and starts believing he doesn't need to practice anymore. When his coach tries to give him advice, he ignores it, thinking, **"I already know how to play."**

But then, Lucas plays against a new opponent and loses badly. His opponent had learned new strategies that Lucas never even considered. If Lucas had kept a **Beginner's Mind**, he would have stayed open to learning instead of assuming he already knew everything.

## Another Example: The Artist Who Kept Improving

Olivia loves drawing. Even though she's good, she still watches tutorials, reads books, and asks other artists for tips. She knows there's always more to learn. Because she stays curious and open-minded, her skills keep improving, while other artists who think they "know enough" stop getting better.

## How to Use Beginner's Mind

To keep learning, remind yourself:

1. **No matter how much you know, there's always more to learn.**
2. **Be curious—ask questions, try new things, and listen to different ideas.**
3. **Don't let success make you overconfident. Stay open to improving.**

## Why This Matters

People who stop learning fall behind. But those who stay curious and open-minded keep growing. If you keep a **Beginner's Mind**, you'll always find new ways to improve, no matter how good you already are.

# Chapter 12: Agility in Learning

Learning isn't just about memorizing facts. It's about being able to **adapt** when things change. Some people struggle when they face something new because they're used to doing things a certain way. Others, however, can adjust quickly and figure things out. This ability is called **Agility in Learning** — being flexible and open to new ways of thinking.

People who learn with agility don't get stuck when things don't go as planned. Instead, they ask, **"What's another way to do this?"** They are quick to adjust, try different approaches, and stay open to change.

### Example: The Math Problem That Didn't Make Sense

Ethan is great at math, but today his teacher is showing a new way to solve problems. It looks completely different from what he's used to. At first, Ethan wants to ignore it and just use the old method. But then he thinks, **"What if this new way is actually easier?"**

Instead of resisting, he tries it. After practicing a few problems, he realizes it's not as confusing as he thought. In fact, it helps him solve problems even faster. By staying flexible, Ethan learns a new skill that makes him even better at math.

## Another Example: The Soccer Player Who Switched Positions

Mia has always played as a forward on her soccer team, but one day, her coach asks her to try defense instead. She isn't sure about it—she's used to scoring goals, not stopping them. At first, she struggles. But instead of giving up, she focuses on learning the new role. She watches how defenders move, listens to her coach, and practices until she gets better.

By being open to change, Mia discovers she's actually great at defense. If she had refused to try something new, she never would have known.

## How to Use Agility in Learning

To become a flexible learner, practice these habits:

1. **Don't be afraid of new methods—try them and see if they work.**
2. **If something isn't working, change your approach.**
3. **Be willing to learn from mistakes and adjust quickly.**

## Why This Matters

The world is always changing, and people who can adapt will always stay ahead. Whether it's school, sports, or everyday life, being flexible in how you learn makes it easier to face new challenges and find success in unexpected places.

# Chapter 13: Mental Flexibility

Some people get stuck when things don't go as expected. They want everything to follow a plan, and when it doesn't, they feel frustrated. But others can **adjust their thinking**, look at problems in new ways, and find solutions no matter what happens. This skill is called **Mental Flexibility** — the ability to change your thinking when needed.

Being mentally flexible helps you stay calm when things don't go your way. It also helps you come up with creative solutions and handle challenges without feeling stuck. Instead of thinking, **"This isn't working, so I give up,"** people with mental flexibility think, **"This isn't working, so what else can I try?"**

## Example: The Science Project That Went Wrong

Noah and his team are building a volcano for the school science fair. They follow the instructions exactly, but when they test it, nothing happens. At first, they feel frustrated. But instead of giving up, they think, **"What if we try a different mix of ingredients?"**

They experiment with different amounts of baking soda and vinegar, making small changes each time. Finally, the volcano erupts just like they wanted. If they had refused to change their approach, they would have been stuck with a project that didn't work.

### Another Example: Changing the Game Plan

Emma's basketball team is losing. The strategy they planned before the game isn't working because the other team is playing differently than expected. Instead of sticking to a plan that isn't working, Emma and her teammates adjust. They change their defense and try a new passing strategy. By staying flexible, they turn the game around and win.

### How to Use Mental Flexibility

To practice thinking in new ways, try these steps:

1. **If something isn't working, don't get frustrated—try a different way.**
2. **Be open to new ideas, even if they seem unusual at first.**
3. **When facing a problem, ask, "What else could I try?"**

### Why This Matters

Life is full of unexpected changes, and people who can adapt will always do better than those who can't. Mental Flexibility helps you solve problems, stay calm when things don't go as planned, and find success in ways you never expected. The more flexible your thinking, the easier it is to handle anything that comes your way.

# Chapter 14: Self-Reflection

Every day, you make choices — some good, some bad. You might ace a test because you studied the right way or lose a game because you didn't practice enough. But how often do you stop and think, **"What did I do well? What could I do better?"** That's what **Self-Reflection** is — taking time to think about your actions and learning from them.

People who practice self-reflection improve faster because they don't just move on from mistakes or successes; they **figure out what worked and what didn't** so they can do better next time.

### Example: The Spelling Bee Comeback

Olivia enters a spelling bee and makes it to the final round. She gets a tough word, spells it wrong, and loses. She feels disappointed, but instead of just forgetting about it, she asks herself:

- **What did I do well?** She stayed calm under pressure.
- **What could I improve?** She realized she struggled with certain types of words.

- **What can I do next time?** She decides to study more word patterns and practice with a friend.

The next year, she enters again — and wins. By reflecting on her past experience, she turned a loss into a lesson.

## Another Example: A Tough Soccer Game

James plays soccer and has a rough game. He missed a few shots, and his passes weren't great. Instead of just feeling bad about it, he thinks through what happened:

- **Why did I miss those shots?** He was rushing too much.
- **Why weren't my passes accurate?** He wasn't looking up before kicking the ball.

Now, he knows what to work on in practice. Instead of repeating the same mistakes, he improves because he took time to reflect.

## How to Use Self-Reflection

To get better at anything, ask yourself after an important event:

1. **What went well?**
2. **What didn't go well?**
3. **What can I do differently next time?**

## Why This Matters

Most people just move on from mistakes without learning from them. But the best athletes, students, and leaders take time to reflect. By thinking about what worked and what didn't, you can improve faster and avoid making the same mistakes over and over. Self-reflection is like having a personal coach in your mind — helping you get better every day.

# Part 3: Decision-Making Like a Genius

Every day, you make decisions—what to eat for breakfast, which game to play, whether to do homework now or later. Some choices are small, but others can have a big impact. **Smart decision-making isn't about luck — it's about using the right thinking tools.** In this part, you'll learn how to weigh your options, think ahead, and make choices that lead to the best results. Whether it's deciding how to spend your time, your energy, or even your money, these tools will help you make **smarter, faster, and more confident decisions.**

# Chapter 15: Cost-Benefit Analysis

Before making a big decision, smart thinkers don't just guess. They **weigh the costs and benefits** to figure out if something is really worth it. This is called **Cost-Benefit Analysis**—a simple way to compare what you'll gain versus what you'll lose before making a choice.

When you do a Cost-Benefit Analysis, you ask:

- **What do I get if I do this?** (The benefits)
- **What do I have to give up?** (The costs)

If the benefits are greater than the costs, it's probably a good decision. If the costs are too high, it might not be worth it.

### Example: Should I Get a Pet?

Liam really wants a dog. He thinks about how fun it would be to play with and take on walks. But before deciding, he does a Cost-Benefit Analysis:

- **Benefits:** He gets a loyal friend, exercise, and fun.
- **Costs:** He has to clean up after it, feed it, and give up time for training.

Liam realizes that while a dog would be great, it's also a big responsibility. He decides to start with a smaller pet, like a fish, to see if he's ready for more responsibility later.

## Another Example: Joining a Club

Emma is thinking about joining the school drama club, but she also plays soccer. She weighs the costs and benefits:

- **Benefits:** She makes new friends, has fun acting, and learns new skills.
- **Costs:** It takes time away from soccer and adds extra rehearsals to her schedule.

After thinking it through, she decides she can balance both. But if the schedule had been too overwhelming, she might have decided to focus on just one activity.

## How to Use Cost-Benefit Analysis

Before making a decision, ask yourself:

1. **What will I gain from this choice?**
2. **What will I have to give up?**
3. **Is the benefit worth the cost?**

## Why This Matters

Many people make decisions without thinking through the consequences. But when you use Cost-Benefit Analysis, you can make smarter choices, avoid regrets, and make sure you're spending your time and energy on things that really matter.

# Chapter 16: Expected Value

Some decisions feel like a gamble — you don't know exactly what will happen, but you have to choose anyway. **Expected Value** helps you make smarter choices by thinking about **the possible outcomes and how likely they are.** Instead of just guessing, you compare the risks and rewards to see which option gives you the best chance of success.

When making a decision, Expected Value helps you ask:

**What could happen if I make this choice?**

**How likely is each outcome?**

**Is this a smart risk, or is it too risky?**

**Example: Should I Enter a Raffle?**

Noah has $5 and sees a raffle where he can win a brand-new bike. A ticket costs $5, and there are 100 tickets in total. He thinks, **"Is this worth it?"**

- **Possible outcome 1:** He wins the bike (1 out of 100 chance).

- **Possible outcome 2:** He doesn't win (99 out of 100 chance).

The Expected Value helps him see that his chances of losing are much higher than his chances of winning. He decides he'd rather **spend his $5 on something that guarantees him a reward,** like a book or a snack.

### Another Example: Studying vs. Guessing on a Test

Sophia has a history test coming up. She's thinking about whether to study or just guess on the questions she doesn't know. She considers the possible outcomes:

- **If she studies, she has a high chance of getting a good grade.**
- **If she doesn't study, she might get lucky, but she'll probably get a bad grade.**

Using Expected Value, Sophia realizes that studying gives her the **best chance of success.** Even though guessing could work, the risk of failing is too high. She studies and feels more confident on test day.

### How to Use Expected Value

When facing a risky decision, ask yourself:

1. **What are the possible outcomes?**
2. **How likely is each outcome?**
3. **Which choice gives me the best overall chance of success?**

### Why This Matters

Many people make decisions based on hope or luck instead of thinking through the risks. But smart thinkers use Expected Value to **see the big picture, avoid bad risks, and make better choices.** The more you think about **probabilities and outcomes,** the better decisions you'll make in life.

# Chapter 17: Opportunity Cost

Every time you make a choice, you're also giving up something else. If you spend an hour playing video games, that's an hour you didn't spend reading, practicing a sport, or hanging out with friends. That trade-off is called **Opportunity Cost**—the hidden cost of every decision.

People often think only about what they're **gaining** when they make a choice, but smart thinkers also ask, **"What am I giving up by choosing this?"** When you understand Opportunity Cost, you can make decisions that **give you the most value for your time, energy, or money.**

### Example: Choosing How to Spend Free Time

Emma has two hours of free time before bed. She can:

1.  Watch a movie.
2.  Read a book she's been wanting to finish.
3.  Work on her art project.

She really wants to watch the movie, but then she thinks about Opportunity Cost. If she chooses the movie, she gives up the chance to finish her book or improve her art skills. Since she only has limited free time, she decides to work on her art—because **that's the choice she'll be happiest about later.**

## Another Example: Spending vs. Saving Money

Liam has $20. He can:

1.  Spend it on snacks and toys right now.
2.  Save it to buy a new skateboard later.

If he spends the money today, the **opportunity cost** is that he won't have enough to buy the skateboard next month. When he thinks about which choice is more valuable to him in the long run, he decides to save.

## How to Use Opportunity Cost

Before making a decision, ask yourself:

1.  **If I choose this, what am I giving up?**
2.  **Which option will matter most to me later?**
3.  **Is there a better way to use my time, energy, or money?**

## Why This Matters

Opportunity Cost helps you see the **real value** of every choice. Instead of just thinking about what you get right now, you learn to think about **what you might be missing out on.** The smartest people make choices that give them the most long-term benefits—not just quick rewards.

# Chapter 18: The Pareto Principle (80/20 Rule)

Not all efforts produce the same results. Some actions give you **way more benefits** than others. The **Pareto Principle**, also called the **80/20 Rule**, says that **80% of results often come from just 20% of the effort.**

This means that instead of working harder on everything, **smart thinkers focus on the few actions that make the biggest difference.**

### Example: Studying Smart, Not Just Studying More

Sofia has a big science test coming up. She could spend hours reading the entire textbook, but instead, she asks: **"What's the most important 20% of the material that will help me the most?"**

She realizes:

- Most test questions come from key topics in her notes.
- Reviewing past quizzes helps her see what she needs to improve.

- Practicing important formulas matters more than reading extra details.

Instead of wasting time on things that won't help much, she **focuses on the key areas** and studies more efficiently.

### Another Example: Improving at Basketball

James wants to get better at basketball. Instead of practicing every single skill equally, he thinks about what will improve his game the fastest. He notices:

- 80% of his missed shots come from bad foot positioning.
- 80% of his turnovers happen when he dribbles too fast.

Instead of randomly practicing, he **focuses on fixing his footwork and dribbling control.** Soon, he sees a huge improvement without spending extra hours on the court.

### How to Use the Pareto Principle

Before spending time or effort on something, ask yourself:

1. **What are the most important 20% of things that will give me the best results?**
2. **Am I wasting time on things that don't matter much?**
3. **How can I focus on the actions that create the biggest improvements?**

### Why This Matters

Most people try to do **everything**, but **successful people focus on the most important things.** By using the 80/20 Rule, you can **work smarter, improve faster, and get better results with less effort.**

# Chapter 19: Loss Aversion

I know I am making the right choice!

People hate losing. In fact, they hate losing so much that they'll often make bad decisions just to avoid it. **Loss Aversion** is the idea that losing something feels worse than gaining something feels good. It's why people sometimes hold onto things they don't need, avoid risks even when they could win, or make choices based on fear instead of logic.

Understanding Loss Aversion helps you **stay calm, think clearly, and make smarter decisions instead of just trying to avoid losses.**

### Example: Keeping a Game You Don't Play

Liam has an old video game he never plays anymore. It just sits on the shelf collecting dust. A friend offers to buy it for $20, but Liam hesitates. **"What if I want to play it again someday?"**

Even though he knows he won't use it, **he feels like he's losing something by selling it.** But when he thinks logically, he realizes:

- He hasn't played the game in over a year.
- He could use the $20 to buy something he actually enjoys.

By overcoming Loss Aversion, Liam makes the smarter choice—selling the game and using the money for something more valuable.

### Another Example: Not Taking a Shot in a Soccer Game

Emma is playing soccer, and she has a chance to take a shot at the goal. But instead of going for it, she hesitates. **"What if I miss?"** she thinks.

Her fear of missing is stronger than her excitement about scoring. But if she never takes the shot, she'll never score at all.

Later, she reminds herself:

**Mistakes are part of learning.**

**The only way to win is to take chances.**

**Even great players miss shots all the time.**

Next time, she takes the shot—and even though she misses, she realizes it wasn't as scary as she thought.

### How to Overcome Loss Aversion

When you feel afraid to lose something, ask yourself:

1. **Am I avoiding this just because I don't want to lose?**
2. **What's the worst that could happen if I take a chance?**
3. **Could I actually gain something by letting go or trying anyway?**

### Why This Matters

Fear of losing can **hold you back from great opportunities.** Whether it's taking a chance, letting go of something you don't need, or making a tough decision, **smart thinkers don't let Loss Aversion control them.** They focus on what they can gain, not just what they might lose.

# Chapter 20: The Eisenhower Matrix

Some people always feel busy but never seem to get important things done. Others know how to focus on what really matters. The difference? **They know how to prioritize.** The **Eisenhower Matrix** is a tool that helps you decide what's truly important and what's just a distraction.

This method sorts tasks into four categories:

1. **Urgent and Important** – Do these first.
2. **Important but Not Urgent** – Plan time for these.
3. **Urgent but Not Important** – Delegate or find a quicker way.
4. **Not Urgent and Not Important** – Avoid or do later.

## Example: Managing Homework and Fun

Noah has homework due tomorrow, a soccer game on Friday, and a new TV show he wants to watch. He uses the Eisenhower Matrix to decide what to do first:

- **Urgent & Important:** Finish tonight's homework.
- **Important but Not Urgent:** Start studying for his test next week.
- **Urgent but Not Important:** Respond to a group chat about weekend plans.
- **Not Urgent & Not Important:** Watch the new TV show (he can do this later).

By focusing on **homework first and scheduling time for studying,** Noah avoids last-minute stress and still has time for fun later.

### Another Example: Organizing a School Project

Emma has a big group project due next week. Instead of waiting until the last minute, she sorts her tasks:

- **Urgent & Important:** Write her part of the project today.
- **Important but Not Urgent:** Review her classmates' work over the weekend.
- **Urgent but Not Important:** Answer a text from a friend asking about the project.
- **Not Urgent & Not Important:** Spend an hour looking at funny videos.

Because she follows the Eisenhower Matrix, she **finishes on time without rushing.**

### How to Use the Eisenhower Matrix

When deciding what to do, ask yourself:

1. **Is this urgent?** (Does it need to be done right away?)
2. **Is this important?** (Will this help me in the long run?)
3. **What should I do first, and what can wait?**

### Why This Matters

Many people waste time on **urgent but unimportant things** instead of focusing on what truly matters. The Eisenhower Matrix helps you **stop feeling overwhelmed, get important things done, and still have time for fun.**

# Part 4: Solving Problems Like a Detective

Every day, you face problems—some big, some small. Maybe you lost something, got stuck on a tough math problem, or couldn't figure out how to beat a level in a video game. **Great problem-solvers don't just guess—they use smart strategies to find solutions.** In this part, you'll learn how to think like a detective, break down problems, and find answers using logic, creativity, and careful thinking. The better you get at solving problems, the easier life becomes.

# Chapter 21: The 5 Whys Technique

When something goes wrong, most people stop at the first explanation they find. But smart thinkers dig deeper. **The 5 Whys Technique** helps you find the real reason behind a problem by asking "Why?" over and over until you reach the root cause.

Instead of fixing **just the surface problem**, this method helps you solve issues **for good** by understanding what really caused them.

### Example: The Late-to-School Mystery

Liam keeps arriving late to school, and his teacher asks him why.

1. **Why were you late?** – "I missed the bus."
2. **Why did you miss the bus?** – "I left the house too late."
3. **Why did you leave late?** – "I took too long getting ready."

4. **Why did you take too long?** – "I couldn't find my homework."

5. **Why couldn't you find your homework?** – "I didn't put it in my backpack the night before."

Now, instead of just telling himself to wake up earlier (which might not solve the real problem), Liam realizes the **true cause**—he needs to pack his backpack before bed.

## Another Example: Fixing a Science Project

Emma's volcano project didn't erupt properly. Instead of giving up, she asks:

1. **Why didn't it work?** – "The mixture didn't bubble up."

2. **Why didn't it bubble?** – "The baking soda and vinegar didn't react enough."

3. **Why didn't they react?** – "Maybe I didn't use the right amounts."

4. **Why didn't I use the right amounts?** – "I didn't measure carefully."

5. **Why didn't I measure carefully?** – "I rushed and didn't double-check my ingredients."

The real problem wasn't the mixture — it was **not taking enough time to measure properly.** Next time, she knows to slow down and check her steps.

## How to Use the 5 Whys Technique

When you face a problem, don't stop at the first answer. Instead:

1. Ask **"Why?"** to find the cause.

2. Keep asking **until you reach the root of the problem.**

3. Fix the real issue, not just the surface mistake.

## Why This Matters

Most people fix problems **too quickly** and never solve the real issue. The 5 Whys Technique helps you **dig deeper, find smarter solutions, and stop problems from happening again.** The better you get at asking "Why?", the better you'll be at solving any challenge.

# Chapter 22: Lateral Thinking

Some problems can't be solved by following the usual steps. **Lateral Thinking** is a way of thinking outside the box—finding creative, unexpected solutions instead of doing things the same old way.

When people use **Lateral Thinking**, they ask:

**"Is there another way to solve this?"**

**"What if I look at the problem from a different angle?"**

**"Can I use something in a way no one has thought of before?"**

Instead of following the obvious path, they find **new and smarter ways** to solve problems.

### Example: The Stuck Truck

A delivery truck gets stuck under a low bridge. The driver and engineers argue about how to get it out—should they break the bridge or take apart the truck?

---

Then, a young boy watching nearby suggests something unexpected: **"Why not just let some air out of the tires?"**

It works. The truck lowers just enough to fit under the bridge. Instead of using force, the boy used **Lateral Thinking** to find a simple, creative solution.

## Another Example: Beating a Difficult Puzzle

Mia is playing a video game with a tricky puzzle. She's supposed to find a key to open a locked door, but she can't find it anywhere.

Instead of searching forever, she stops and asks, **"What if there's another way?"**

She checks her inventory and finds a heavy object. Instead of unlocking the door, she uses the object to break through a weak part of the wall—and it works. She beat the puzzle by **thinking differently.**

## How to Use Lateral Thinking

To solve problems creatively, try this:

1. **Challenge normal thinking.** Ask, "Is there another way?"
2. **Look at the problem from different angles.** What would happen if you reversed the situation?
3. **Try unusual ideas.** Even silly ideas might lead to a great solution.

## Why This Matters

Many people get stuck because they only think in **one direction**. But problems don't always have just one solution. Lateral Thinking helps you **see more possibilities, solve tricky problems, and come up with ideas others might never think of.** The more you practice, the better you'll be at finding creative solutions in any situation.

# Chapter 23: The Feynman Technique

Some people study for hours but still struggle to understand what they're learning. Others seem to master things quickly. What's the difference? The people who learn best don't just memorize facts—they make sure they truly **understand** them. One of the best ways to do this is called **The Feynman Technique** — a simple method for learning anything faster and better.

This technique is based on a simple idea: **If you can explain something in a way a younger kid could understand, you really know it.** If you can't, you probably don't understand it as well as you think.

### Example: Learning a Science Topic

Emma is learning about gravity in school. She reads the definition in her textbook, but it still feels confusing. Instead of just reading it over and over, she tries the Feynman Technique:

1. **She explains it as if teaching a younger sibling.** She says, "Gravity is what makes things fall down instead of floating away."

2. **She finds gaps in her understanding.** Her little brother asks, "But why do things fall down?" She realizes she doesn't fully know, so she looks it up.

3. **She simplifies it even more.** She tries again: "Gravity is a force that pulls things toward the Earth."

4. **She reviews and improves.** Now, she really understands it and doesn't just memorize words from a textbook.

## Another Example: Studying for a Math Test

Liam is struggling with fractions. Instead of just practicing problems over and over, he tries to **teach the concept to himself** as if explaining it to a friend.

- First, he writes down what he knows: "A fraction is part of a whole."
- Then, he tries to make it simpler: "It's like cutting a pizza—each slice is a fraction of the whole pizza."
- Finally, he tests himself by solving a problem and explaining why each step works.

By explaining the concept in simple terms, Liam **understands it deeply** instead of just memorizing formulas.

## How to Use the Feynman Technique

To learn anything faster, follow these steps:

1. **Try to explain it simply, as if teaching a younger kid.**
2. **Find the parts you don't fully understand.**
3. **Look up answers and simplify your explanation.**
4. **Keep practicing until you can explain it clearly.**

## Why This Matters

Most people think they understand something just because they recognize the words. But real learning happens when you can **explain an idea in your own words.** The Feynman Technique helps you learn faster, remember longer, and truly understand any subject — not just for a test, but for life.

# Chapter 24: Heuristic Problem Solving

Some problems take a long time to solve, but others can be solved quickly with **shortcuts.** No, not cheating — **smart strategies that help you find a good answer fast.** These shortcuts are called **heuristics**—simple thinking techniques that help you make quick, effective decisions without overcomplicating things.

Heuristics don't always lead to a perfect solution, but they help you get a **good enough answer quickly** — which is often all you need.

### Example: Guessing the Answer on a Test

Liam is taking a multiple-choice test and gets stuck on a question. He doesn't have time to think through every possibility, so he uses a heuristic:

- **First, he eliminates answers that are obviously wrong.**

- **Then, he looks for clues in the other questions to help him decide.**
- **Finally, he makes an educated guess instead of wasting time.**

Instead of getting stuck, Liam **uses a quick strategy to improve his chances of picking the right answer.**

## Another Example: Finding a Lost Phone

Mia loses her phone. Instead of searching **everywhere** in the house, she uses a heuristic:

- **She retraces her steps.** Where was she last?
- **She checks the most common places first.** Her desk, her backpack, the couch.
- **She asks herself where she would usually put it.**

By following a smart process instead of panicking, Mia **finds her phone much faster.**

## How to Use Heuristic Problem Solving

When facing a tricky problem, try these steps:

1. **Eliminate bad options first.** Don't waste time on things that won't work.
2. **Look for patterns or clues.** Past experiences can guide you.
3. **Use a quick strategy that makes sense.** It doesn't have to be perfect—just good enough.

## Why This Matters

Some problems take deep thinking, but many can be solved **faster and easier with the right mental shortcuts.** Heuristics help you **save time, make smarter choices, and avoid getting stuck.** The more you practice, the faster you'll be at solving problems in school, sports, and everyday life.

# Chapter 25: The Scientific Method

Some people make guesses and hope they're right. Scientists, inventors, and great problem-solvers do something smarter — they **test their ideas** using the **Scientific Method.** This step-by-step way of thinking helps you find the truth, solve problems, and make better decisions based on **facts** instead of just opinions or guesses.

The Scientific Method follows these steps:

1. **Ask a question.** What are you trying to figure out?
2. **Make a hypothesis.** This is your best guess at the answer.
3. **Test it.** Do an experiment or gather information.
4. **Analyze the results.** Did your test prove your guess right or wrong?
5. **Adjust and try again.** If your guess was wrong, make a new one and test again.

## Example: The Mystery of the Dying Plants

Emma's plants keep dying, and she doesn't know why. Instead of just guessing, she uses the Scientific Method.

1. **Ask a question:** Why are my plants dying?
2. **Make a hypothesis:** Maybe they aren't getting enough sunlight.
3. **Test it:** She moves one plant to a sunnier spot and leaves another in the same place.
4. **Analyze the results:** The plant in the sun grows better.
5. **Adjust and try again:** She moves all her plants to sunnier areas and watches them thrive.

By testing instead of assuming, Emma **finds the real solution** instead of making random changes.

## Another Example: Fixing a Slow Internet Connection

Liam's video game keeps lagging, and he's frustrated. Instead of complaining, he **tests different solutions.**

1. **Ask a question:** Why is my game lagging?
2. **Make a hypothesis:** Maybe the Wi-Fi signal is weak.
3. **Test it:** He moves closer to the router and tries again.
4. **Analyze the results:** The game runs smoother.
5. **Adjust and try again:** He realizes sitting closer helps, so he starts playing near the router.

Instead of just hoping the problem fixes itself, Liam **finds the real cause and makes a smart change.**

## How to Use the Scientific Method

When solving a problem, ask yourself:

1. **What am I trying to figure out?**
2. **What do I think the answer is?**
3. **How can I test it?**
4. **What happened? Did it work?**
5. **What should I change and try next?**

## Why This Matters

Most people **guess** their way through problems, but the best thinkers **test their ideas and learn from the results.** The Scientific Method helps you **find real answers, solve problems faster, and make decisions based on facts—not just guesses.**

# Chapter 26: Hypothesis Testing

Have you ever made a guess about something and then tested it to see if you were right? That's called **Hypothesis Testing** — a way to check if an idea is true before believing it. Instead of just assuming something, smart thinkers **test their ideas to make sure they actually work.**

A **hypothesis** is just a fancy word for an educated guess. It's what you **think** will happen, but you don't know for sure yet. **Testing your guess helps you find the truth.**

### Example: Does Wearing Lucky Socks Help?

Noah has a big soccer game and wears his "lucky socks." His team wins, and he thinks, **"My socks made us win!"** But did they really? He decides to test his hypothesis:

1. **Make a hypothesis:** "If I wear my lucky socks, my team will always win."

2. **Test it:** He wears the socks in the next game—but his team loses.

3. **Check the results:** He realizes **the socks don't actually affect the game.** It's his skill and teamwork that matter, not the socks.

By testing his idea instead of just believing it, Noah **discovers the truth.**

## Another Example: What's the Best Way to Study?

Emma wants to improve her test scores. She hears that **studying in the morning** might help, but she usually studies at night. Instead of just assuming one way is better, she tests it:

1. **Make a hypothesis:** "If I study in the morning, I will remember more."
2. **Test it:** She studies at night for one test and in the morning for another.
3. **Check the results:** She compares her scores and realizes she actually remembers things better in the morning.

Now, she knows what works best for her, instead of just guessing.

## How to Use Hypothesis Testing

When you're unsure about something, try this:

1. **Make a hypothesis.** What do you *think* is true?
2. **Test it.** Try different ways and compare results.
3. **Check the outcome.** Did it work the way you thought? If not, what's the real answer?

## Why This Matters

Many people **believe things just because they seem true** — but the smartest people **test their ideas before trusting them.** Hypothesis Testing helps you **separate fact from fiction, solve problems faster, and make better decisions.** If you want to think like a scientist, always test before you believe!

# Chapter 27: Root Cause Analysis

When something goes wrong, many people try to fix the problem **quickly** without figuring out what really caused it. But if you don't fix the **root cause**, the problem will keep happening. **Root Cause Analysis** is a way of digging deeper to find the real reason behind a problem so you can solve it for good.

Instead of just asking, **"How do I fix this?"** ask, **"Why did this happen in the first place?"**

## Example: The Case of the Broken Pencil

Lucas keeps breaking his pencils during class. He sharpens them again and again, but they keep snapping. Instead of just grabbing a new pencil every time, he decides to find out why.

1. **Identify the problem:** His pencils keep breaking.
2. **Ask why it's happening:** He notices he's pressing too hard while writing.
3. **Find the root cause:** He realizes he holds his pencil too tightly.

4. **Solve the real problem:** He relaxes his grip, and now his pencils last much longer.

If he had just kept sharpening them, he would have **never fixed the real issue.**

## Another Example: The Late Homework Mystery

Mia keeps turning in her homework late, and it's starting to affect her grades. At first, she thinks, **"I just need to work faster."** But instead of rushing, she decides to find the root cause.

1. **Identify the problem:** Homework is always late.
2. **Ask why it's happening:** She realizes she gets distracted by her phone.
3. **Find the root cause:** She studies in a noisy place, so it's easy to lose focus.
4. **Solve the real problem:** She moves to a quiet spot and puts her phone away while working.

By fixing the real issue, Mia stops struggling with late homework instead of **just trying to work faster.**

## How to Use Root Cause Analysis

When a problem happens, ask yourself:

1. **What is the problem?**
2. **Why did it happen?**
3. **What caused that?** (Keep asking "why" until you find the root cause.)
4. **How can I fix the real issue so it doesn't happen again?**

## Why This Matters

Many people **only fix surface-level problems,** so the same issues keep happening. Root Cause Analysis helps you **solve problems permanently** by finding what's really causing them. Instead of fixing the same mistakes over and over, you can **solve them once and for all.**

# Part 5: Winning Strategies for Big Thinkers

Some people seem to make great decisions and solve problems quickly, while others struggle. What's their secret? **They think strategically.** Strategic thinkers don't just react to what's happening now—they plan ahead, consider different possibilities, and make smart moves. In this part, you'll learn how to think like a chess master, plan for the future, and stay one step ahead in school, sports, and life.

# Chapter 28: The OODA Loop

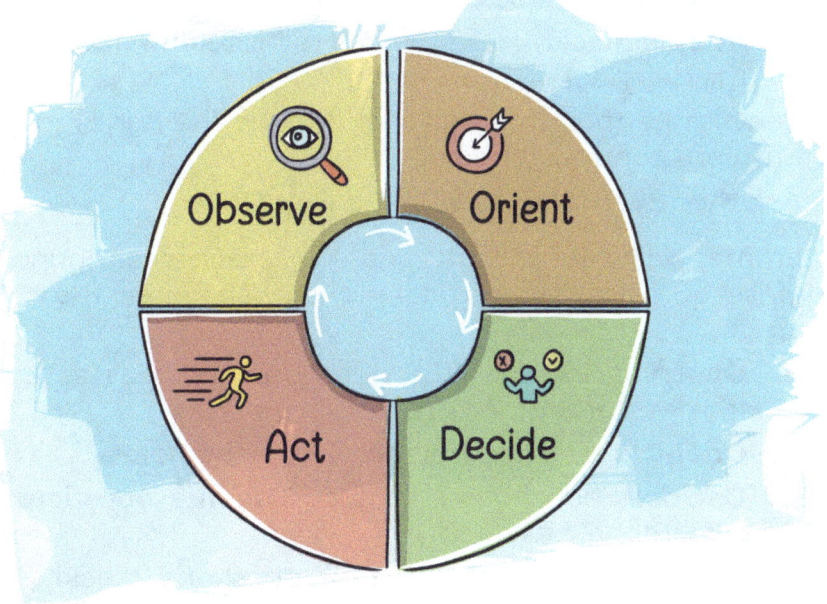

In fast-moving situations, some people freeze or panic. Others make quick, smart decisions that help them win. The secret? They use the **OODA Loop**—a four-step process that helps people react fast and make the right choices.

OODA stands for:

1. **Observe** – Look at what's happening.
2. **Orient** – Think about what it means.
3. **Decide** – Choose your best move.
4. **Act** – Do it quickly.

This cycle repeats over and over, helping you **stay ahead** in any situation.

### Example: A Soccer Game Decision

Liam is playing soccer, and a defender is running toward him. Instead of panicking, he quickly goes through the OODA Loop:

1. **Observe:** He sees the defender coming fast.

2. **Orient:** He remembers that his teammate is open on the left.

3. **Decide:** He chooses to pass the ball.

4. **Act:** He quickly kicks the ball to his teammate, avoiding the defender.

Because he thought quickly and made the right move, his team keeps control of the ball.

## Another Example: Handling a Pop Quiz

Emma walks into class, and her teacher announces a surprise quiz. Instead of freaking out, she uses the OODA Loop:

1. **Observe:** She sees the questions and realizes they're from yesterday's lesson.

2. **Orient:** She remembers she took good notes.

3. **Decide:** She chooses to focus on the questions she remembers best first.

4. **Act:** She answers the easy questions quickly, then spends more time on the harder ones.

By thinking fast and staying calm, she does her best on the quiz.

## How to Use the OODA Loop

When you need to make a quick decision, follow these steps:

1. **Observe:** Pay attention to what's happening around you.

2. **Orient:** Think about what it means and what your options are.

3. **Decide:** Choose the best action.

4. **Act:** Do it fast, then repeat if needed.

## Why This Matters

The OODA Loop is used by **athletes, pilots, and military leaders** to make fast, smart choices under pressure. The better you get at using it, the quicker you'll be at **reacting, adjusting, and making great decisions — no matter what comes your way.**

# Chapter 29: Scenario Planning

Things don't always go as planned. That's why smart thinkers **prepare for different possibilities** instead of hoping everything works out perfectly. **Scenario Planning** is a way of thinking ahead by asking, *"What might happen?"* and *"What will I do if it does?"*

Instead of creating just one plan, you imagine a few different futures — **the good, the bad, and the unexpected** — so, you're ready no matter what happens.

## Example: Preparing for a Class Presentation

Sofia has a big class presentation coming up. She wants to make sure everything goes well, so she plans for different scenarios:

- **Best case:** Everything works perfectly—she speaks clearly, her slides work, and the class listens.
- **Worst case:** The projector doesn't work.
- **Surprise case:** Her teacher cuts the presentation time in half.

Because Sofia thought ahead, she's ready for all of it. She prints out backup notes in case the slides fail and prepares a shorter version just in case. When something does go wrong— her slides won't load—she calmly switches to her printed notes and still does a great job.

## Another Example: Planning a School Field Trip

Noah is helping organize a school field trip. He doesn't just hope for sunny weather and perfect timing. Instead, he helps the group prepare for:

- **Rainy weather:** They bring umbrellas and raincoats.
- **Traffic delays:** They leave early and bring activities for the bus ride.
- **Someone forgetting lunch:** They pack extra snacks just in case.

By thinking through different situations ahead of time, Noah and his classmates **enjoy the day without panic or problems.**

## How to Use Scenario Planning

Before something important, ask yourself:

1. **What are a few different things that could happen?**
2. **What would I do in each case?**
3. **What can I prepare ahead of time to make things easier?**

## Why This Matters

Most people make only one plan and get stuck when something changes. Scenario Planning helps you think like a leader—**ready for anything, calm under pressure, and always one step ahead.** When you plan for many outcomes, you'll never be caught off guard.

# Chapter 30: Risk Management

Every choice has some kind of risk. Risk is the chance that something might go wrong or not turn out the way you hoped. But that doesn't mean you should avoid all risks. **Smart thinkers learn how to manage risk** — to notice it, think it through, and make safer, smarter decisions. This is called **Risk Management**.

Instead of asking, *"How do I avoid all risk?"*, people who manage risk ask, *"How can I be smart about this risk?"* They **look at what might go wrong**, how likely it is, and **what they can do to prepare** or protect themselves.

### Example: Planning a Group Project

Emma and her classmates are working on a group project. They decide to divide the work evenly. But Emma realizes there's a risk: what if someone forgets to do their part?

Instead of hoping everything goes smoothly, she manages the risk:

- She sets up a check-in halfway through the week.
- She makes sure everyone knows what they're doing.
- She has a backup plan in case someone gets sick or misses school.

Because she thought ahead, the group stays on track—even when one student forgets to email their part.

## Another Example: Training for a Swim Meet

Liam has an important swim meet coming up. He wants to do his best, but there are risks—he might get too tired before the final lap, he could mess up his turn, or he might lose focus under pressure. Instead of just hoping for the best, he manages these risks:

- He practices pacing himself so he doesn't burn out too quickly.
- He works on perfecting his turns during practice to avoid mistakes in the race.
- He visualizes the race in his head, imagining himself staying calm and focused.

Because he prepared for possible problems, Liam feels more confident on race day—and even when things don't go perfectly, he knows how to adjust and keep going.

## How to Use Risk Management

Whenever you make a decision, try this:
1. **What could go wrong?**
2. **How likely is that to happen?**
3. **What can I do to reduce the risk or prepare for it?**

## Why This Matters

Taking risks is part of life — but managing them helps you avoid big mistakes, stay calm in tough situations, and make better choices. **Risk Management doesn't mean avoiding challenges. It means being ready for them.** And the more prepared you are, the braver and smarter your decisions will be.

# Chapter 31: Long-Term Thinking

Some decisions seem small now but have a big impact later. **Long-Term Thinking** means looking beyond what feels good **right now** and making choices that will help you in the future. Instead of asking, **"What do I want today?"** smart thinkers ask, **"What will matter most later?"**

People who think long-term don't just focus on quick rewards. They make choices that help them **grow, improve, and succeed over time.**

### Example: Training for a Marathon

Emma loves running, and she dreams of completing a marathon one day. But running 26 miles is a huge challenge. She knows she can't just wake up and do it—she has to train over time.

- She starts by running short distances and slowly increases her endurance.
- Even when training feels tough, she reminds herself that progress takes time.

- Instead of quitting when she doesn't see results right away, she trusts the process.

Months later, she's running longer distances with ease. Because she **thought ahead and stuck with her plan**, she reaches her goal.

## Another Example: Learning to Play an Instrument

Noah wants to learn the violin, but at first, it sounds terrible. He could quit and try something easier, but he remembers that learning anything new takes time.

- He practices a little bit every day, even when progress is slow.
- He sets a goal to play a full song in three months.
- He reminds himself that every great musician started as a beginner.

By staying patient and thinking about **his future skills instead of his current struggles**, Noah improves—and after a few months, he's playing songs he once thought were impossible.

## How to Use Long-Term Thinking

Before making a decision, ask yourself:

1. **Will this choice help me in the future, or just right now?**
2. **If I stick with this, where will I be in a few months or years?**
3. **Is short-term discomfort worth the long-term success?**

## Why This Matters

Many people quit too soon because they **only focus on today.** But success comes from thinking ahead, staying patient, and making choices that will **pay off in the future.** The best goals take time, and the smartest thinkers **focus on where they want to be, not just where they are now.**

# Chapter 32: The Hedgehog Concept

Some people try to be good at everything but never become great at anything. Others focus on **what they do best** and become truly successful. The **Hedgehog Concept** is about finding **your one big strength** and using it to succeed instead of trying to do too many things at once.

This idea comes from an old fable about a fox and a hedgehog. The fox is clever and tries lots of tricky ways to catch the hedgehog, but the hedgehog has **one simple, powerful defense** — it curls into a spiky ball, and the fox never wins. The lesson? **Being really good at one thing is often more powerful than trying to do everything.**

## Example: Choosing a Sport

Liam enjoys playing different sports, but he realizes he's especially talented at swimming. Instead of stretching himself thin by joining five different teams, he decides to focus on swimming.

- He practices more and becomes one of the strongest swimmers in his school.
- He enjoys it because it's something he's naturally good at.
- He improves faster than if he had divided his time between many different sports.

By focusing on **his best strength**, Liam reaches his full potential instead of being average at everything.

### Another Example: Picking the Right Extracurricular Activity

Sofia likes music, dance, and art, but she's especially passionate about singing. Instead of signing up for too many activities, she chooses to focus on choir.

- She takes lessons and practices every day.
- She gets better faster because she's putting all her effort into one area.
- She has more fun and feels more confident because she's doing what she loves most.

Because she **focused on what she's best at**, Sofia improves more than if she had split her time between too many hobbies.

### How to Use the Hedgehog Concept

To find your strength, ask yourself:
1. **What do I love doing?**
2. **What am I naturally good at?**
3. **What could I get even better at if I focused on it?**

### Why This Matters

Many people try to do too many things at once and never reach their full potential. The Hedgehog Concept teaches you that **focusing on what you do best** helps you improve faster, enjoy what you do, and achieve more in the long run. When you find **your** strength, lean into it — and you'll go further than you ever thought possible.

# Chapter 33: Red Teaming

Our arguments look great. Are we ready for the debate?

Not yet. Let's pretend to be our opponents and think how they would argue.

Most people assume their ideas are correct and never question them. But smart thinkers **test their own ideas** to find weaknesses before anyone else does. **Red Teaming** is a strategy where you look at your own plan **as if you were trying to prove it wrong.** This helps you spot mistakes, improve your thinking, and avoid problems before they happen.

Instead of asking, **"Why is my idea right?"**, Red Teaming helps you ask, **"What if I'm wrong?"**

## Example: Preparing for a Debate

Emma is getting ready for a debate in class. She has strong arguments, but instead of just practicing her speech, she tries Red Teaming.

- She **pretends to be her opponent** and thinks about how they might argue against her points.
- She finds weaknesses in her own arguments and improves them.

- She prepares strong counterpoints so she won't be caught off guard.

When the debate happens, Emma is ready for every challenge because she already tested her own ideas.

## Another Example: Planning a Community Fundraiser

Noah's neighborhood is organizing a fundraiser, and he's in charge of planning. Before finalizing everything, he uses Red Teaming:

- He **imagines possible problems**—What if not enough people show up? What if the location is too small? What if it rains?

- He **creates solutions** for each issue—He spreads the word early, picks a bigger space, and plans for a backup indoor location.

- Because he tested his plan, **he fixes problems before they happen.**

On the day of the event, everything runs smoothly—not because he was lucky, but because he **thought ahead and challenged his own plan.**

## How to Use Red Teaming

Before finalizing an idea, ask yourself:

1. **What could go wrong?**
2. **If I were arguing against myself, what weaknesses would I find?**
3. **How can I fix those weaknesses before they become real problems?**

## Why This Matters

Most people don't like questioning their own ideas, but Red Teaming makes you **stronger, smarter, and more prepared.** Whether you're making a big decision, presenting an idea, or solving a problem, **testing yourself first helps you succeed when it really matters.**

# Chapter 34: Competitive Analysis

Success isn't just about working hard—it's also about **paying attention to what others are doing. Competitive Analysis** is the skill of studying others to learn from their successes and mistakes. It helps you improve by seeing what works, what doesn't, and how you can do things better.

Instead of just focusing on yourself, **smart thinkers look at the competition, ask smart questions, and find ways to improve.**

## Example: Running a Bake Sale

Emma and her friends are organizing a bake sale to raise money for a local charity. Before deciding what to sell, she visits a bakery to see which treats people buy the most. She also checks last year's bake sale and notices that:

- Cookies sold out quickly.
- The fancy cupcakes looked great but didn't sell as well.
- Some booths had long lines, while others had almost no customers.

By **learning from past sales and real customers**, Emma and her team decide to make more cookies and set up a faster checkout process. Because of this, they raise more money than they expected.

## Another Example: Launching a School Newspaper

Noah wants to start a school newspaper, but instead of guessing what students want to read, he studies other school newspapers:

- He sees what types of articles get the most attention.
- He asks students what they'd like to read about.
- He notices what didn't work in past newspapers and avoids those mistakes.

Because Noah **analyzes what others have done before**, his school newspaper is a success — students love reading it because it's focused on what they actually care about.

## How to Use Competitive Analysis

Before starting a project, ask yourself:

1. **Who has done something similar before?**
2. **What worked well for them?**
3. **What mistakes did they make that I can avoid?**

## Why This Matters

Many people try to succeed **without learning from others**, which means they make unnecessary mistakes. **Competitive Analysis helps you improve faster by studying what already works.** Instead of starting from scratch, you can **build on what others have already figured out** — giving yourself a big advantage.

# Chapter 35: Contingency Planning

No matter how well you plan, unexpected things can still happen. **Contingency Planning** means preparing backup plans so you're ready for anything. Instead of hoping everything goes perfectly, **smart thinkers ask, "What will I do if things go wrong?"**

Having a **Plan B (and sometimes a Plan C)** helps you stay calm and in control, even when surprises come your way.

## Example: Organizing an Outdoor Event

Sofia is planning a neighborhood picnic. She has everything ready — food, games, and decorations. But then she thinks, **"What if it rains?"** Instead of waiting to see what happens, she makes a contingency plan:

- She finds an indoor space nearby that they can use if needed.
- She checks the weather forecast the day before.
- She tells everyone about the backup plan in advance.

On the day of the picnic, a storm rolls in, but Sofia doesn't panic. She **switches to Plan B**, and the picnic moves indoors without problems.

### Another Example: Preparing for a Big Test

Liam has been studying hard for a history test, but he realizes something could still go wrong. He asks himself: **"What if I forget some of the key facts during the test?"**

To prepare, he makes a contingency plan:

- He creates a simple study guide with the most important information.
- He practices explaining the material in his own words so he understands it better.
- He gets a good night's sleep to help his memory.

On test day, he feels nervous at first, but because he **prepared for challenges**, he remembers what he studied and does well.

### How to Use Contingency Planning

Before an important event, ask yourself:

1. **What could go wrong?**
2. **What's my backup plan if it happens?**
3. **How can I prepare now so I don't panic later?**

### Why This Matters

Many people **hope for the best but don't prepare for the worst.** Contingency Planning helps you **stay in control, handle surprises, and keep moving forward—even when things don't go as expected.** When you have a backup plan, nothing can stop you.

# Part 6: Communicating Like a Pro

Being smart isn't just about thinking well — it's also about **expressing your ideas clearly** and **understanding others.** Good communication helps you share your thoughts, listen better, and work well with people. In this part, you'll learn how to ask great questions, explain things simply, and make sure people really understand what you mean. Whether you're talking to friends, teachers, or family, these skills will help you connect, learn, and succeed.

# Chapter 36: The 5W Model

When you want to understand something deeply, asking the right questions is key. The **5W Model** is a simple way to get all the important details by asking:

- **Who?**
- **What?**
- **Where?**
- **When?**
- **Why?**

These five questions help you **get the full picture of any situation** and make sure you don't miss key details.

## Example: Investigating a Missing Library Book

Emma's class library is missing a book, and the teacher wants to find out what happened. Instead of making random guesses, Emma asks the 5W questions:

- **Who** checked out the book last?
- **What** was the book about?
- **Where** was it last seen?
- **When** did it go missing?
- **Why** might someone have taken it without returning it?

By asking these questions, she pieces together the clues and helps find the missing book.

## Another Example: Planning a School Fundraiser

Noah and his classmates want to organize a fundraiser, but they need to figure out the details. Using the 5W Model, they ask:

- **Who** will be involved? (Students, teachers, parents?)
- **What** type of fundraiser should it be? (Bake sale, car wash, raffle?)
- **Where** will it take place? (School gym, playground, or outside?)
- **When** should it happen? (During lunch, after school, or on the weekend?)
- **Why** are they raising money? (To buy books, support a charity, or fund a class trip?)

By answering these questions, they make a solid plan and ensure the fundraiser is a success.

## How to Use the 5W Model

When trying to understand something, ask yourself:

1. **Who is involved?**
2. **What is happening?**
3. **Where is it taking place?**
4. **When did (or will) it happen?**
5. **Why is it important?**

## Why This Matters

Many people jump to conclusions without gathering enough information. The 5W Model helps you **ask better questions, understand situations fully, and think more clearly.** The more you use it, the better you'll be at finding answers and making smart decisions.

# Chapter 37: Active Listening

Most people hear words when someone talks, but **few people really listen. Active Listening** means paying full attention, understanding what's being said, and showing the speaker that you care about their words. It helps you learn more, build stronger relationships, and avoid misunderstandings.

Instead of just waiting for your turn to talk, **active listeners focus on the speaker, think about what's being said, and respond in a thoughtful way.**

## Example: Understanding a Friend's Problem

Sofia's friend is upset and starts telling her about a problem. Instead of interrupting or thinking about what to say next, Sofia practices Active Listening:

- She **looks at her friend** to show she's paying attention.
- She **doesn't interrupt** and lets her friend finish speaking.

- She **nods and asks questions** to show she understands: "That sounds frustrating. What happened next?"
- She **repeats the key points**: "So, you felt left out when they didn't invite you?"

Because Sofia listens carefully, her friend feels heard and understood.

## Another Example: Learning from a Grandparent

Liam's grandfather is telling a story about his childhood. Liam could just sit there and nod, but instead, he practices Active Listening:

- He **asks questions** to learn more: "What was school like back then?"
- He **paraphrases** what he hears: "So you had to walk everywhere because there were no buses?"
- He **avoids distractions** like his phone so he can focus.

Because Liam listens actively, he learns a lot and has a meaningful conversation with his grandfather.

## How to Use Active Listening

When talking to someone, try this:

1. **Look at the speaker and give them your full attention.**
2. **Don't interrupt—let them finish their thoughts.**
3. **Ask questions to understand more deeply.**
4. **Repeat or summarize key points to show you're listening.**

## Why This Matters

Good listeners understand more, make fewer mistakes, and build better relationships. **Active Listening helps you connect with people, learn faster, and become a better communicator.** The more you practice, the more people will appreciate talking to you.

# Chapter 38: Feedback Framework

Getting feedback can be hard—sometimes it feels like criticism, and nobody likes to be told they did something wrong. But smart thinkers know that **feedback is a tool for growth.** The **Feedback Framework** helps you give and receive advice in a way that makes learning easier, not discouraging.

Instead of seeing feedback as something negative, **think of it as a way to improve faster.**

## Example: Receiving Feedback on an Essay

Emma works hard on an essay and feels proud of it. When her teacher returns it with comments, she notices suggestions for improvement. Instead of feeling discouraged, she follows the Feedback Framework:

- **Listen with an open mind** – She reminds herself that feedback isn't about failure; it's about learning.
- **Ask questions** – She doesn't just look at the mistakes; she asks her teacher, "How can I make this sentence clearer?"

- **Apply what she learns** – She rewrites her essay using the advice, and next time, her writing is even better.

By seeing feedback as **help, not criticism,** Emma improves instead of getting frustrated.

## Another Example: Giving Feedback to a Sibling

Noah's younger brother is learning to cook and asks him to taste the soup he made. Noah doesn't want to hurt his feelings, but he also wants to be honest. Instead of just saying, "It's bad," he uses the Feedback Framework:

- **Start with something positive** – "The soup smells really good!"
- **Give a helpful suggestion** – "It might taste even better with a little more salt."
- **End with encouragement** – "You're getting really good at cooking!"

Because of this, his brother doesn't feel bad — he feels motivated to improve.

## How to Use the Feedback Framework

When receiving feedback:
1. **Stay open-minded and don't take it personally.**
2. **Ask questions to understand how to improve.**
3. **Apply the advice to get better.**

When giving feedback:
1. **Start with something positive.**
2. **Give clear, helpful advice.**
3. **Encourage the person to keep improving.**

## Why This Matters

Many people ignore feedback or get upset by it, but smart thinkers **use it to grow.** Whether you're giving or receiving advice, the Feedback Framework helps you **improve faster, communicate better, and help others do the same.**

# Chapter 39: Empathy Mapping

Good communication isn't just about talking — it's also about **understanding how others feel. Empathy Mapping** is a way to put yourself in someone else's shoes so you can see the world from their perspective. It helps you become a better listener, solve conflicts, and build stronger relationships.

Instead of just thinking about your own feelings, **Empathy Mapping helps you ask, "What is this person thinking? What are they feeling?"**

### Example: Understanding a Friend's Bad Mood

Sofia's best friend, Ava, has been acting quiet all day. At first, Sofia feels upset—did she do something wrong? But instead of jumping to conclusions, she uses Empathy Mapping:

- **What is Ava thinking?** Maybe she has something on her mind.
- **What is Ava feeling?** She seems sad or stressed.
- **What is Ava seeing?** Maybe she had a tough morning at home.

- **What is Ava hearing?** Did someone say something that hurt her feelings?

Sofia realizes Ava's mood might not have anything to do with her. So instead of getting upset, she simply asks, **"Hey, is everything okay?"** Ava opens up about a problem at home, and Sofia is able to support her.

## Another Example: Handling a Difficult Teacher

Noah's history teacher is strict and gives a lot of homework. At first, Noah thinks, **"This teacher just wants to make my life hard!"** But when he tries Empathy Mapping, he sees things differently:

- **What is my teacher thinking?** He wants students to learn and be prepared.
- **What is my teacher feeling?** Maybe he's frustrated when students don't do their work.
- **What is my teacher seeing?** A classroom full of kids who might not be paying attention.
- **What is my teacher hearing?** Complaints instead of effort.

By understanding his teacher's point of view, Noah realizes the teacher isn't trying to be mean—he just cares about students doing their best. Instead of complaining, Noah asks, **"What's the best way to study for this?"** His teacher appreciates the effort, and Noah finds the work easier to handle.

## How to Use Empathy Mapping

When someone is upset, difficult, or acting differently, ask yourself:

1. **What might they be thinking?**
2. **What emotions are they feeling?**
3. **What are they seeing in their world?**
4. **What are they hearing from others?**

## Why This Matters

Many conflicts happen because people don't try to understand each other. **Empathy Mapping helps you see things from someone else's point of view, making you a better friend, teammate, and communicator.** The more you practice, the easier it becomes to connect with others and handle tough situations.

# Chapter 40: The Elevator Pitch

Sometimes you only have a few seconds to explain an idea, and you have to make it **clear, interesting, and easy to understand.** That's where the **Elevator Pitch** comes in. It's a short, simple way to share your idea in the time it takes to ride an elevator—about 30 seconds to one minute.

Whether you're sharing a project, introducing yourself, or explaining a plan, an Elevator Pitch helps you **get to the point quickly without confusing people.**

## Example: Explaining a School Project

Sofia's teacher asks her to explain her science fair project in front of the class. Instead of rambling, Sofia uses an Elevator Pitch:

- She starts with a **hook**: "Did you know plants can grow without soil?"
- She clearly explains the idea: "My project shows how plants can grow using only water and nutrients."

- She ends with why it matters: "This could help people grow food in places where soil isn't available."

In less than a minute, everyone understands her project — and they're interested.

## Another Example: Sharing an Idea with a Principal

Noah wants to start a recycling program at his school, but he knows the principal is busy. He plans an Elevator Pitch before their quick hallway meeting:

- **Hook**: "What if our school could reduce waste and help the environment at the same time?"
- **Idea**: "I want to start a student-led recycling program with bins in each classroom."
- **Why it matters**: "It'll teach responsibility, protect the planet, and make our school cleaner."

The principal likes the idea and asks to hear more later—because Noah explained it **clearly and quickly.**

## How to Create an Elevator Pitch

When you need to share an idea fast, follow these steps:

1. **Start with a hook**—a surprising fact or question to get attention.
2. **Explain your idea simply**—no big words or long stories.
3. **End with why it matters**—show why people should care.

## Why This Matters

You won't always have time for a long explanation. The Elevator Pitch helps you **get your point across fast, stay clear, and make people want to hear more.** It's a skill that helps in school, in conversations, and in life—because great ideas only matter if people understand them.

# Chapter 41: Reframing

Change the frame, change the perspective

Sometimes a problem feels big and frustrating—until you **look at it in a different way.** That's what **Reframing** is all about. It means **changing how you see a situation** so you can understand it better, feel more in control, or find a new solution.

The situation stays the same—but your point of view changes. And that small shift can make a big difference.

### Example: Turning a Chore into a Challenge

Sofia has to clean her room, and she's not excited about it. At first, she thinks, **"This is so boring."** But then she decides to reframe it:

- Instead of seeing it as a boring chore, she sees it as a challenge.
- She sets a timer and tries to beat her best time.
- She turns on music and makes it a game.

Now the task feels fun and satisfying—and she gets it done faster.

## Another Example: Seeing Feedback Differently

Noah gets feedback on an art project. His teacher points out some things he could improve. At first, he feels discouraged. But then he reframes the situation:

- Instead of thinking, "I failed," he thinks, "This is a chance to get better."
- He remembers that even professional artists get feedback.
- He focuses on what he can learn, not what went wrong.

By changing how he sees the feedback, he feels motivated instead of upset—and his next project turns out even better.

## How to Use Reframing

When something feels difficult or negative, ask yourself:

1. **Is there another way to look at this?**
2. **Can I turn this into a challenge or learning moment?**
3. **What's something positive I can find in this situation?**

## Why This Matters

Your thoughts shape how you feel and what you do. Reframing helps you **stay calm, think clearly, and turn problems into opportunities.** When you change your perspective, you often change the outcome too. Smart thinkers don't just react—they **choose how to see the world.**

# Chapter 42: The Socratic Method

One of the best ways to get smarter isn't by giving answers—it's by asking **better questions.** The **Socratic Method** is a way of learning by asking thoughtful questions to explore ideas, challenge beliefs, and uncover the truth.

It's named after **Socrates**, a famous thinker from ancient Greece who didn't give long speeches — he just kept asking questions until people figured things out for themselves.

The Socratic Method helps you think more deeply, spot weak ideas, and understand things clearly — **not just memorize facts, but truly understand them.**

### Example: Digging Deeper in a Class Discussion

Sofia is in a class discussion about fairness. A student says, "It's unfair that some people get more than others."

Instead of just agreeing or disagreeing, Sofia uses the Socratic Method:

- She asks, "What do we mean by fair?"
- Then, "Is it always unfair when people have different things?"

- And, "Are there times when differences are okay—or even necessary?"

Her questions make the whole class think more deeply, and the discussion becomes more thoughtful and interesting.

## Another Example: Questioning a Big Decision

Noah is thinking about quitting an after-school activity because it feels hard. Before making a decision, he uses the Socratic Method to question himself:

- "Why do I want to quit?"
- "What part feels hard—and why?"
- "Is there something I could change to make it better?"
- "What might I regret if I stop now?"

These questions help him realize he doesn't want to quit—he just needs to talk to his coach and ask for help with one part of the activity.

## How to Use the Socratic Method

Whenever you face a tricky idea or decision, try this:

1. **Ask a question about the topic.**
2. **Then ask a deeper question about your answer.**
3. **Keep going until you understand more clearly.**

## Why This Matters

Quick answers aren't always the best ones. The Socratic Method helps you **slow down, ask better questions, and discover deeper truths.** It turns you into a thoughtful thinker who doesn't just accept ideas—but understands them.

# Part 7: Outsmarting Your Own Brain

Your brain is amazing—it helps you think, learn, and solve problems. But sometimes, it also plays tricks on you. Without even realizing it, you might make decisions based on feelings, guesses, or habits instead of logic and facts. In this part, you'll learn how to spot those brain tricks (called **biases**) and train your mind to be clearer, calmer, and smarter. Think of it like becoming the coach of your own brain—so it works *for* you, not *against* you.

# Chapter 43: Cognitive Bias Awareness

Everyone is going to the skateboard park, it's the best!

Are you sure that place is safe? It's really close to a dangerous area!

Your brain has shortcuts it uses to make quick decisions. Most of the time, that's helpful. But sometimes, these shortcuts cause you to make **bad choices without realizing it.** These mental mistakes are called **cognitive biases**, and everyone has them—even adults!

Being aware of your biases doesn't mean you're wrong or silly—it just means you're human. But if you can **spot those tricky thoughts**, you can make smarter decisions.

### Example: Believing the Loudest Voice

Sofia is in a group project, and one person keeps talking loudly and confidently, even when they're wrong. The group agrees with that person, even though Emma has better ideas. Why? It's a **bias** called the *authority bias* — people often trust the loudest or most confident voice, even if it isn't the smartest.

Once Sofia realizes this, she speaks up and shares her idea. The group listens, and they end up with a much better project.

## Another Example: Choosing What's Familiar

Noah always picks the same book series at the library. When someone suggests a new one, he says, "No thanks, I won't like it." That's the **familiarity bias**—your brain likes what it already knows.

Later, he decides to give the new series a try and ends up loving it. He realizes his brain was holding him back just because the new book felt unfamiliar.

## How to Outsmart Cognitive Biases

Start by asking yourself:

1. **Am I choosing this just because it's familiar, easy, or popular?**
2. **Am I ignoring better options because of a gut feeling or habit?**
3. **What would I think if I looked at this from a different point of view?**

## Why This Matters

Cognitive biases can quietly lead you away from the smartest choice. But once you learn to **spot those mental tricks**, you can pause, rethink, and choose more wisely. Great thinkers aren't perfect—they're just better at noticing when their brains are trying to take a shortcut.

# Chapter 44: Anchoring Bias

Imagine you're shopping for a backpack. The first one you see costs $80. The next one is $50, and suddenly it seems like a great deal—even if it's still more than you wanted to spend. That's called **Anchoring Bias** — when your brain grabs onto the first number, idea, or piece of information it sees, and compares everything else to it, even if it's not the most helpful starting point.

**Anchoring Bias** happens because our brains like to **lock onto the first thing we hear or see** — and that "anchor" affects how we think about everything after it.

## Example: Judging a Story by the First Sentence

Sofia reads a news article that begins with, "This is the worst storm our town has ever seen." Before she even finishes the story, her brain already believes it's the worst — just because that's what she saw first. But later, when she checks the facts, she finds out there have been stronger storms in the past.

The first sentence anchored her thinking. Once she knew that, she was able to step back and think more clearly.

## Another Example: Choosing a Topic for an Essay

Noah's teacher gives a list of possible essay topics. The first topic says "Why school uniforms are important." Without reading the others, Noah decides that's the best one. But later, he realizes there was a topic he liked much more—he just didn't notice it because his brain got stuck on the first one.

He learns to slow down and look at **all** the options before deciding, so he doesn't let the first idea take over his thinking.

## How to Outsmart Anchoring Bias

When making a decision, try this:

1. **Ask yourself, "Am I only thinking this because it was the first thing I saw or heard?"**
2. **Look at all the options before choosing.**
3. **Compare based on facts, not just first impressions.**

## Why This Matters

Anchoring Bias can lead you to **make quick decisions without thinking deeply.** By noticing when you're stuck on the first idea, number, or option, you give yourself the power to pause, explore more choices, and make smarter decisions. Smart thinkers don't let the *first* thing be the *only* thing they consider.

# Chapter 45: Confirmation Bias

Have you ever believed something so strongly that you only noticed the things that proved you right — and ignored everything that didn't? That's called **Confirmation Bias.** It's when your brain looks for evidence that supports what you already believe, even if that belief isn't fully true.

This bias feels sneaky because you don't even realize it's happening. But smart thinkers learn to **ask questions, explore both sides, and stay open to new information— even when it doesn't match what they expected.**

### Example: Picking a Science Fair Idea

Sofia believes that plants grow faster with music. She's so sure of it that when she does her science fair project, she **only pays attention to the plants that grew well**—and ignores the ones that didn't.

When her teacher asks her, "What about the plants that didn't grow with music?" Sofia realizes she was only seeing what she wanted to see. Next time, she pays attention to **all the results**, not just the ones that match her belief.

## Another Example: Forming an Opinion About a Classmate

Noah hears that a new student is rude. So, on the first day, he watches for signs of bad behavior—and sure enough, when the student doesn't say hello, Noah thinks, "See? Rude." But later, he finds out the student was just nervous and shy.

Noah's brain was using **confirmation bias**—looking for proof to match the story he already believed. Once he saw the full picture, his opinion changed.

### How to Outsmart Confirmation Bias

When you're forming an opinion or making a choice, ask yourself:

1. **Am I only looking at the side that supports what I already believe?**
2. **What would I think if I saw the opposite evidence?**
3. **Have I truly explored both sides of the issue?**

### Why This Matters

Confirmation Bias can trick you into thinking you're right—even when you're not. But by staying curious, open-minded, and willing to look at all the facts, you can **find the truth instead of just proving yourself right.** Great thinkers don't just ask, "How am I right?" — they ask, **"Could I be wrong?"**

# Chapter 46: Availability Heuristic

When your brain makes a decision quickly based on the first example that pops into your mind, that's called the **Availability Heuristic.** It's like your brain saying, "If I can remember it easily, it must be important or true!" But just because something is easy to remember doesn't mean it happens often — or that it's the right answer.

This thinking shortcut can lead to mistakes, especially when what comes to mind **isn't the full story.**

### Example: Judging What's Dangerous

Sofia watches a movie about a plane crash. The next day, her class is learning about transportation safety, and she says, "Planes are the most dangerous way to travel!"

But her teacher explains that plane crashes are actually very rare — **they just stick in our memory because they're dramatic.** Car accidents happen way more often, but they don't make the news as much.

---

Sofia realizes her brain was using the **Availability Heuristic** — remembering what was easy to picture, not what was most common.

### Another Example: Picking a Topic for a Report

Noah is writing a report about famous inventors. The first person who comes to mind is Thomas Edison, because he's heard that name many times. So he says, "I'll just do it on Edison."

But then he decides to look deeper and finds out about **other inventors who made amazing things**—people he hadn't heard about yet. He ends up choosing someone even more interesting because he didn't just go with the first name that popped into his head.

### How to Outsmart the Availability Heuristic

When making a choice or forming an opinion, ask yourself:

1. **Am I just choosing the first thing I remember?**
2. **Is this idea actually common or just memorable?**
3. **What does the real evidence say—not just what I've seen or heard lately?**

### Why This Matters

Your brain loves shortcuts, but they don't always lead to the truth. The Availability Heuristic can make something **seem** important just because it's easy to recall. But smart thinkers slow down and check the facts. They ask, "Is this really true—or just the first thing I thought of?"

# Chapter 47: Social Proof

Have you ever done something just because **everyone else was doing it?** Maybe you joined a line without knowing what it was for, or picked a popular book just because lots of people were reading it. That's called **Social Proof**—when your brain assumes that if many people are doing something, it must be the right choice.

Social Proof can be helpful sometimes, but it can also lead you to **follow the crowd without thinking for yourself.**

### Example: Choosing a Book to Read

Sofia goes to the library and sees a shelf labeled "Most Popular Books." She grabs one without reading the summary, just because "everyone else is reading it." But halfway through, she realizes she's not enjoying it at all.

She picked it based on **what others liked**, not on what *she* likes. Next time, she reads the descriptions and picks a book that matches her interests—even if it's not the most popular one.

## Another Example: Joining a Group Decision

Noah and his classmates are choosing a name for their project team. One person suggests a name, and everyone agrees quickly—even though Noah has a better idea. He stays quiet, thinking, **"If everyone else likes it, maybe I'm wrong."**

But later, another student says, "I actually didn't like that name either." They all realize they had just gone along with the group. Noah learns that **speaking up, even when you're the only one with a different idea, can lead to better choices.**

## How to Outsmart Social Proof

Before following the crowd, ask yourself:

1. **Am I choosing this because I like it—or just because others are?**
2. **What do *I* actually think about this?**
3. **Would I make the same choice if no one else had?**

## Why This Matters

Social Proof can make you feel safe by following the crowd—but it can also stop you from thinking for yourself. Smart thinkers don't just copy others. They pause, ask questions, and make **choices that match their own values, ideas, and goals.** It's okay to stand out if it means you're being true to yourself.

# Chapter 48: Grit and Resilience

Sometimes things are hard. You might struggle with a new subject, make a mistake, or face something that feels impossible. But smart thinkers don't give up when things get tough — they use **grit and resilience.**

**Grit** means sticking with something even when it's difficult. **Resilience** means bouncing back when something goes wrong. Together, they help you keep going, **even when you feel like quitting.**

## Example: Learning a New Skill

Sofia wants to learn how to draw realistic faces. At first, her sketches look nothing like what she imagined. She feels frustrated and thinks, "Maybe I'm just not good at this."

But instead of quitting, she shows grit:

- She practices every day, even when it's hard.
- She looks at her old drawings to see how far she's come.
- She keeps going—one mistake at a time, one improvement at a time.

After weeks of effort, her drawings are much better. She didn't need to be perfect—she just needed to keep trying.

## Another Example: Facing a Setback

Noah works hard on a science project but doesn't win a prize. He feels disappointed and thinks all his work was wasted. But after a few days, he chooses to be resilient:

- He looks at what he did well and what he could improve.
- He asks his teacher for feedback.
- He decides to try again next time — with new ideas and more confidence.

His project didn't win, but his **growth mindset** did.

## How to Build Grit and Resilience

1. **Expect challenges.** Struggling doesn't mean you're failing — it means you're growing.
2. **Keep showing up.** Small steps every day lead to big changes over time.
3. **Learn from setbacks.** Ask, "What can I do better next time?"

## Why This Matters

The most successful people in the world aren't the ones who never fall — they're the ones who **get back up, again and again.** Grit and resilience give you the power to face challenges, stay strong, and reach your goals — even when the road gets bumpy. When you don't quit, **you win.**

# Chapter 49: Habit Formation

Your habits are the things you do over and over—sometimes without even thinking. Brushing your teeth, tying your shoes, or saying "thank you" are all examples of habits. Some habits are helpful, and some can get in your way. **Habit Formation** is the process of creating good habits that stick—and breaking the ones that don't help you.

Smart thinkers know that **small actions done often become powerful over time.**

### Example: Starting a Reading Habit

Sofia wants to read more, but she always forgets or says she'll do it later. So she decides to build a habit:

- She starts reading **just five minutes a day** after brushing her teeth.
- She leaves her book on her pillow so she sees it every night.
- After a few weeks, reading feels automatic—she doesn't even have to remind herself.

By keeping it simple and repeating it daily, she builds a strong reading habit that **becomes part of her routine.**

## Another Example: Breaking a Distraction Habit

Noah finds himself checking his tablet every time he tries to do homework. He wants to focus better, so he makes a plan:

- He leaves his tablet in another room while studying.
- He sets a timer for 20 minutes to work without distractions.
- He rewards himself with break time after finishing a task.

After practicing this routine for a few weeks, his brain starts to expect focus time when he sits down—**his distraction habit gets replaced by a concentration habit.**

## How to Build (or Break) a Habit

To build a habit:

1. **Start small**—pick one easy thing you can do every day.
2. **Link it to something you already do** (like after breakfast or before bed).
3. **Repeat it consistently** until it becomes automatic.

To break a habit:

1. **Notice when and where it happens.**
2. **Replace it** with something more helpful.
3. **Remove the triggers** that cause it (like turning off notifications).

## Why This Matters

Habits shape your life—even the tiny ones. By building good habits and breaking bad ones, you take control of your choices instead of letting your brain run on autopilot. Smart thinkers don't rely on willpower alone—they **build systems that make success automatic.**

# Chapter 50: Emotional Regulation

Everyone feels big emotions sometimes—like anger, sadness, excitement, or fear. That's totally normal. But smart thinkers know how to **manage their emotions instead of letting emotions manage them.** That skill is called **Emotional Regulation** — the ability to notice your feelings, stay calm, and make good choices, even when you're upset or overwhelmed.

Emotions are like signals: they tell you something is going on. But you don't have to act on them right away. **You can pause, breathe, and choose how to respond.**

### Example: Staying Calm During a Disagreement

Sofia is working on a group project when someone says her idea is "not good." She feels a wave of anger and wants to snap back. But she takes a deep breath, counts to five, and says calmly, "Can you tell me what you didn't like about it?"

Because she stayed in control, the group keeps working well together, and they find a better solution as a team. **She felt her emotions—but didn't let them take over.**

### Another Example: Dealing with Disappointment

Noah tries out for something he really wanted and doesn't make it. He feels sad and frustrated. Instead of pretending he's fine or quitting everything, he uses Emotional Regulation:

- He **talks to someone he trusts** about how he feels.
- He **gives himself time** to feel disappointed without giving up.
- He **reminds himself** that failure is part of learning—and that he can try again.

By managing his emotions, Noah bounces back stronger and more motivated.

### How to Practice Emotional Regulation

1. **Pause and name the feeling.** ("I'm feeling angry," or "I'm nervous.")
2. **Take a few deep breaths** to slow your body and mind.
3. **Choose your response** instead of reacting too fast.
4. **Talk it out or write it down** if you need to let the feelings out safely.

### Why This Matters

Everyone feels emotions, but not everyone **knows how to handle them.** Emotional Regulation helps you stay steady, make wiser decisions, and handle tough moments without losing control. Smart thinkers don't ignore feelings—they **listen to them, manage them, and then move forward.**

# Conclusion: Your Brain Is Your Superpower

Congratulations! You've just learned 50 powerful thinking tools that most people don't even know exist. These are the same tools used by inventors, scientists, leaders, and problem-solvers all around the world. And now, **you have them too.**

You've learned how to think clearly, make smarter decisions, solve tough problems, and bounce back from mistakes. You know how to ask better questions, stay calm under pressure, and see situations from different angles. You've learned how to outsmart distractions, manage your emotions, and build better habits.

But here's the most important part: **You don't have to be perfect.** Great thinkers aren't people who never make mistakes — they're people who **learn from their mistakes, keep improving, and never stop asking, "What's the smart way to handle this?"**

Your brain is like a muscle. The more you use these thinking tools, the stronger your brain becomes. Some days you'll forget. Some days you'll get it wrong. That's okay. Every time you try again, you're building a brain that's sharper, calmer, and ready for anything.

Keep this book as a guide. Flip through it when you're stuck. Use it to remind yourself that **you already know how to outsmart challenges** — you just have to choose to use what you've learned.

Whether you're solving a puzzle, writing a story, talking to a friend, or facing a big decision, remember this: **You are capable. You are curious. And you are training your mind to be one of the strongest tools in the world.**

So, keep thinking. Keep learning. And most of all—**keep growing.**

Because smart thinking isn't about knowing all the answers. It's about **knowing how to find them.**

# Extras for Super Thinkers!
# Appendix 1: Quick Mental Model Guide

Use this guide to quickly remember the 50 mental models in this book. Each one is a powerful tool to help you **think smarter, solve problems, and make better decisions!**

## Part 1: Smart Thinking Basics

1. **First Principles Thinking** – Thinking like a scientist! Breaking big problems into small, easy pieces.
2. **Second-Order Thinking** – Thinking ahead: what happens *next* if you make a choice?
3. **Occam's Razor** – The simplest answer is *usually* right!
4. **Hanlon's Razor** – People aren't always mean on purpose — sometimes, they just make mistakes!
5. **Inversion** – Thinking backward to solve tricky problems.
6. **The Circle of Competence** – What are you really good at? And what do you need to learn?

## Part 2: Learning Superpowers

7. **The Learning Curve** – Learning new things feels hard at first, but it gets easier!
8. **Feedback Loops** – How practice makes perfect.
9. **Meta-Learning** – Learning *how* to learn faster.
10. **Incremental Growth** – Small steps = BIG progress!

**11. Shoshin (Beginner's Mind)** – Staying curious like a kid, even when you're an expert.

**12. Agility in Learning** – How to adapt when things change.

**13. Mental Flexibility** – Thinking in new ways when things don't go as planned.

**14. Self-Reflection** – Learning from mistakes without feeling bad.

## Part 3: Decision-Making Like a Genius

**15. Cost-Benefit Analysis** – Is something *really* worth it?

**16. Expected Value** – Making smart choices by thinking about the future.

**17. Opportunity Cost** – Choosing one thing means giving up something else—make it count!

**18. The Pareto Principle (80/20 Rule)** – 20% of your effort gets 80% of the results!

**19. Loss Aversion** – Why losing feels worse than winning feels good—and how to stay calm.

**20. The Eisenhower Matrix** – What's important vs. what's just urgent?

## Part 4: Solving Problems Like a Detective

**21. The 5 Whys Technique** – Asking "why?" five times to find the real problem.

**22. Lateral Thinking** – Thinking outside the box!

**23. The Feynman Technique** – Teach it to a five-year-old, and you'll understand it better!

**24. Heuristic Problem Solving** – Fast thinking vs. slow thinking.

**25. The Scientific Method** – How scientists figure things out.

**26. Hypothesis Testing** – Guess, test, and learn!

**27. Root Cause Analysis** – Finding the real reason something went wrong.

## Part 5: Winning Strategies for Big Thinkers

**28. The OODA Loop** – Observe, Orient, Decide, Act—quick thinking in action!

**29. Scenario Planning** – What if things don't go as expected?

**30. Risk Management** – Should you take the risk or play it safe?

**31. Long-Term Thinking** – Thinking about the future *before* making choices today.

**32. The Hedgehog Concept** – Finding *your* superpower!

**33. Red Teaming** – What would the *opposite* side say?

**34. Competitive Analysis** – Learning from the best!

**35. Contingency Planning** – Having a backup plan.

## Part 6: Communicating Like a Pro

**36. The 5W Model** – Who, What, Where, When, Why? Asking the right questions!

**37. Active Listening** – How to *really* hear what people are saying.

**38. Feedback Framework** – Giving and getting helpful advice.

**39. Empathy Mapping** – Stepping into someone else's shoes.

**40. The Elevator Pitch** – Explaining big ideas in just a few words.

**41. Reframing** – Looking at things from a different angle.

**42. The Socratic Method** – Asking questions to get smarter!

## Part 7: Outsmarting Your Own Brain

**43. Cognitive Bias Awareness** – When your brain plays tricks on you!

**44. Anchoring Bias** – Why first impressions matter more than they should.

**45. Confirmation Bias** – Seeing what you *want* to see, not what's real.

**46. Availability Heuristic** – Just because you remember it doesn't mean it's common.

**47. Social Proof** – Why we follow the crowd (even when it's wrong!).

**48. Grit and Resilience** – Keep going, even when things are tough!

**49. Habit Formation** – How to build great habits (and break bad ones).

**50. Emotional Regulation** – Staying cool under pressure.

This is your **ultimate thinking toolkit.** Whenever you face a challenge, look through this list and pick the right mental model to help you **think faster, smarter, and more clearly.** The more you practice, the stronger your thinking skills will become!

# Appendix 2: Mental Models Game – 15 Real-Life Challenges

Now it's time to put your **mental models** to the test! Below are 15 real-life challenges. Try to figure out which **mental model(s)** would help in each situation. Then, check the solutions to see if you got it right!

## Challenge 1: The Late Homework Problem

You keep turning in your homework late. It's not because you don't want to do it, but something always seems to go wrong. Sometimes you forget, sometimes you run out of time. **How can you fix this for good?**

### Solution: Root Cause Analysis + Habit Formation

Instead of just trying harder, ask, **"Why does this keep happening?"** Maybe you always start too late, or distractions get in the way. Once you find the real cause, you can build a habit—like always finishing homework before dinner.

## Challenge 2: The Lost Phone Mystery

You keep losing your phone. Every time, you spend 10 minutes searching for it. **How can you make sure this doesn't happen again?**

### Solution: The 5 Whys Technique + Habit Formation

Ask, **"Why do I keep losing my phone?"** Maybe you always put it in different places. If that's the case, create a habit of always placing it in the same spot—like a special basket by the door.

## Challenge 3: The Messy Locker

Your school locker is a disaster. Every time you open it, things fall out, and it takes forever to find what you need. **How can you fix this?**

### Solution: The Eisenhower Matrix

Sort your items: **urgent and important** (books, homework), **important but not urgent** (extra supplies), and **not important** (old papers, trash). A simple system—like keeping books on one shelf and supplies in a bin — will help you stay organized.

## Challenge 4: The Best Friend Misunderstanding

Your friend didn't respond to your message. You immediately think they're mad at you. **What mental model helps you think more clearly?**

### Solution: Hanlon's Razor + Reframing

Instead of assuming the worst, remember that **people usually aren't trying to be mean**—they might just be busy! Reframe the situation: "Maybe they're just having a busy day."

## Challenge 5: The Tricky Test Question

You're taking a multiple-choice test, and you don't know the answer. **What should you do?**

### Solution: Heuristic Problem Solving

Use quick thinking! Eliminate obviously wrong answers first, then make the best choice based on logic.

## Challenge 6: The Big School Project

You have a giant project due in a month, but you don't know where to start. **How can you make it manageable?**

### Solution: First Principles Thinking + Incremental Growth

Break the project into small pieces. Instead of thinking, "I have to write a whole report," think, **"First, I need to research. Then, I'll outline. Then, I'll write one section at a time."**

## Challenge 7: The Impossible Puzzle

You're stuck on a really hard problem. No matter what you try, nothing works. **What should you do?**

### Solution: Lateral Thinking + The Feynman Technique

Try thinking in a completely different way. What if you **solve it backward**? What if you **explain it to a younger sibling**? A fresh perspective can reveal new solutions.

## Challenge 8: The Big Decision

You're trying to decide whether to join the chess club or the drama club. **How do you choose?**

### Solution: Opportunity Cost + The Pareto Principle

Think about what you **gain and give up** with each choice. Also, ask: **"Which activity will give me the most benefits for the effort I put in?"**

## Challenge 9: The Rainy Day Picnic

You and your friends planned a picnic, but now the weather forecast says it might rain. **What do you do?**

### Solution: Scenario Planning + Contingency Planning

Plan for different possibilities! If it rains, is there an indoor backup plan? If the weather clears up, can you still go? Thinking ahead means you're ready for anything.

## Challenge 10: The "Lucky" Socks

Your team won a game while you wore your lucky socks. Now you think they're magic. **Is this logical?**

### Solution: Hypothesis Testing + The Scientific Method

Test it! Try playing without the socks and see if your skill changes. Chances are, your hard work—not the socks—made the difference.

## Challenge 11: The Group Project Dilemma

Your group keeps getting stuck on decisions because no one wants to disagree. **How can you improve the discussions?**

### Solution: Red Teaming + The Socratic Method

Encourage different viewpoints! Ask, **"What would someone who disagrees say?"** or **"What if we're wrong?"** These questions help you make smarter choices.

## Challenge 12: The Overloaded Schedule

You have school, sports, homework, and family time, and now you're exhausted. **What's the best way to manage your time?**

### Solution: The Eisenhower Matrix + The Pareto Principle

Prioritize! Focus on **important things first** and drop things that don't matter as much. Sometimes, doing **less** leads to better results.

## Challenge 13: The Viral Trend

Everyone at school is talking about a new trend, and you feel pressured to follow along—even though you're not really interested. **What mental model helps you think for yourself?**

### Solution: Social Proof + Reframing

Just because lots of people are doing something doesn't mean **you have to.** Reframe the situation: **"Do I actually like this, or am I just following the crowd?"**

## Challenge 14: The Hard-to-Believe Story

A friend tells you something shocking they heard online. Before believing it, **what should you do?**

### Solution: Confirmation Bias + Cognitive Bias Awareness

Check if you're only believing it because it matches what you already think. Look for real evidence—not just one side of the story.

## Challenge 15: The Fear of Failing

You want to try out for something new, but you're afraid you won't be good enough. **What's the best mindset to have?**

### Solution: Grit and Resilience + Growth Mindset

Failure isn't the opposite of success—it's part of success! Every expert started as a beginner. Keep going, even when things feel tough.

## Final Thoughts

Mental models help you **think smarter in real life.** The more you practice using them, the better you'll get at solving problems, making decisions, and **outsmarting challenges.**

How many did you get right? Keep practicing, and soon these thinking tools will become second nature!

# Appendix 3: Top 10 Thinking Hacks

Want to think faster, learn better, and outsmart challenges? Here are **10 of the best thinking hacks** to help you make smarter decisions, solve tricky problems, and stay ahead in any situation.

**1. Break Big Problems into Tiny Pieces (First Principles Thinking)**

When something feels overwhelming, don't panic! **Break it down into smaller, easier parts.** Instead of thinking, *"This is too hard,"* ask, *"What's the first small step I can take?"*

**Example:** Need to write a long essay? Start by just brainstorming ideas for five minutes.

**2. Think One Step Ahead (Second-Order Thinking)**

Don't just ask, *"What happens if I do this?"* Ask, *"And then what happens next?"* Smart thinkers **look ahead** so they don't get surprised later.

**Example:** Staying up late seems fun — until you realize you'll be exhausted for your test tomorrow!

**3. Choose the 20% That Matters Most (Pareto Principle)**

Not everything is equally important. **Most results come from a small part of your effort.** Focus on what gives you the biggest benefit.

**Example:** Studying **key ideas** instead of every little detail helps you learn faster.

### 4. Ask "Why?" Five Times (The 5 Whys Technique)

Instead of guessing, **dig deep to find the real cause of a problem.** Keep asking *"Why?"* until you find the root cause.

**Example:** You're late to school. Why? You woke up late. Why? You slept too late. Why? You were on your phone. Why? You didn't set a bedtime. **Now you know what to fix!**

### 5. Don't Assume—Test It! (Hypothesis Testing)

Before believing something, **test if it's really true.** Smart thinkers don't assume—they check the facts.

**Example:** Do "lucky socks" actually help you win, or is it just your practice paying off?

### 6. Stop Worrying, Start Planning (Scenario Planning + Contingency Planning)

Instead of stressing about *"What if something goes wrong?"* ask, *"What's my backup plan?"* Preparing for different possibilities makes you **feel in control.**

**Example:** What if it rains on the day of your outdoor event? **Have an indoor plan ready!**

### 7. Change How You See the Problem (Reframing)

Instead of saying *"This is too hard,"* ask, *"How can I make this easier?"* A new perspective can **turn a problem into an opportunity.**

**Example:** A boring chore? Turn it into a race or challenge!

### 8. Slow Down and Think (Cognitive Bias Awareness)

Your brain loves shortcuts, but they're not always right! **Pause and check your thinking before making quick decisions.**

**Example:** Just because everyone believes something doesn't make it true—**check the facts!**

### 9. Keep Going, Even When It's Hard (Grit and Resilience)

Success isn't about never failing—it's about **never giving up.** If you keep trying, you'll always improve.

**Example:** Struggling with a new skill? **That's how learning works! Keep practicing, and you'll get there.**

## 10. Ask Better Questions (The Socratic Method)

Smart thinkers **don't just memorize answers—they ask great questions.** The more you question, the more you learn.

**Example:** Instead of just accepting an idea, ask, **"Why is this true?"** or **"Is there another way?"**

### Final Thought

Thinking isn't just something you do — it's a **superpower you can train.** The more you use these hacks, the **sharper, faster, and stronger your mind** will become.

So, next time you face a challenge, **don't just react — think!**

# Here's another book by Quinn Voss that you might like

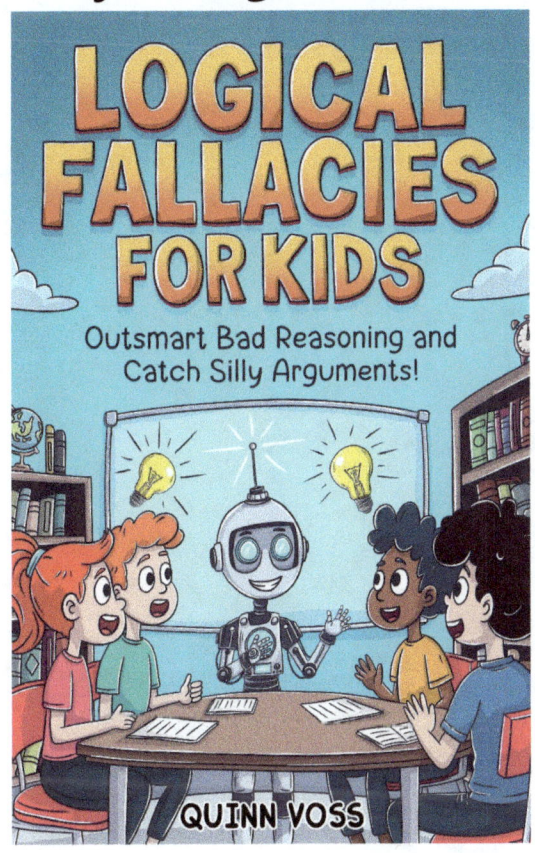

www.ingramcontent.com/pod-product-compliance
Lightning Source LLC
Chambersburg PA
CBHW061806120626
46550CB00005B/2165